POMPILIA

"POMPILIA"
Bust by: Pen Browning
Courtesy of the English Poetry Collection,
Wellesley College Library,
Wellesley, Massachusetts

P O M P I L I A

A Feminist Reading of

Robert Browning's

The Ring and the Book

Ann P. Brady

Ohio University Press

Athens

Ohio University Press books are printed on acid-free paper. ∞

Brady, Ann P.
   Pompilia: a feminist reading of Robert Browning's The ring and the
book / Ann P. Brady.
      p.   cm.
   Bibliography: p.
   Includes index.
   ISBN 0-8214-0886-0
   1. Browning, Robert, 1812-1889. Ring and the book.
2. Franceschini, Guido, conte, 1657-1698, in fiction, drama, poetry, etc.
3. Franceschini, Pompilia, 1680-1698, in fiction, drama, poetry, etc.
4. Feminism in literature. 5. Misogyny in literature. 6. Patriarchy in
literature. 7. Victims of crimes in literature. 8. Crime and criminals in
literature. 9. Italy in literature.
   I. Title.
PR4219.B7 1988   88-1733
821'.8—dc 19   CIP

For My Mother, Josephine E. Brady

CONTENTS

Acknowledgments   ix

Foreword: Apologia Pro Vita Sua   1

1. Introduction: The Filthy Rags of Speech   11

2. *Honoris Causa:* Misogyny in Church and Society   27

3. The First Experimentalists   63

4. The Equilateral Triangle   99

5. Conclusion: Robert Browning, Victorian Feminist   123

Notes   135

Index   145

ACKNOWLEDGMENTS

Acknowledgment is due to Richard D. Altick and the Yale University Press for permission to use Richard D. Altick's edition of *The Ring and the Book*; to Balliol College Library for access to the Old Yellow Book; to the British Library for access to Robert Browning's manuscript of *The Ring and the Book*; to the Margaret Clapp Library at Wellesley College for permission to use a photograph of Pen Browning's bust of Pompilia, and to the Browning Institute for furnishing the photograph; to Virago for several quotations from *Not in God's Image: Women in History*, edited by Julia O'Faolain and Lauro Martines; to Dr. Claudia Stillman Franks, author of *Beyond the Well of Loneliness: The Fiction of Radclyffe Hall*, for her invaluable counsel and prodigious help in preparing the first manuscript of this book; to my sister and friend, Dr. Dolores Brady, for her countless encouragements, consultations, and practical assistance.

FOREWORD

Apologia Pro Vita Sua

ROBERT BROWNING was no feminist in any conventionally definable sense. In 1885, near the end of his long career, he was actually considering a five-act play against women's suffrage.[1] But Browning is a web of contradictions. The poet so concerned about the liberation of Italy in the 1850s deplores the idea of home rule for Ireland in the 1880s. The man who lasted barely more than one term at the London University was chagrined at his son's failure to gain admittance to Balliol College, and positively bitter at his ignominious expulsion from Christ Church in 1870, thus forfeiting the Oxford degree so dear to his father's heart. Nor is it a simple matter of barnacled age. The champion of personal independence and drive always had lived off the sustenance of others, first his father, then his wife, both in precarious enough circumstances themselves: Robert Browning, senior, having given up a lucrative career in the West Indies because of his revulsion to slavery; Elizabeth Barrett Barrett having been disinherited by her father because of her marriage. These two, parent and spouse, knew the price and paid the cost of their moral decisions. Part of their financial anguish, moreover, concerned the exigency of supporting the poet in suitable style. Such personal opaqueness in so perceptive an observer and so staunch a reactor to human blindness and injustice gives one pause. In this examination of *The Ring and the Book*[2] I hope to illuminate a powerful and penetrating feminism that I think is manifested throughout Browning's masterpiece. However, I am only too aware how some of my points could be obfuscated by incidents and attitudes in the poet's own contradictory life.

Roma King has noted that Browning's seventeenth-century Italian murder story is a penetrating comment on the poet's own times: "His awareness of the limits of human reason and his distrust of those values codified in social customs and institutions reflect more nearly the skeptical mood of the nineteenth than of the seventeenth century."[3] My study concurs with this, and attempts to highlight some of the value contrasts between Robert Browning and his culture as manifested in his treatment of the Franceschini murder trial. Yet in his own life we find him concurring with his culture on points that seem inconsistent with certain typically Browningesque affirmations about human life.

In the love letters (1845-46) he defends with gusto the institution of dueling and the right to revenge killing as a redress for injustice.[4] Elizabeth Barrett is shocked at the revelation, responding the same day in dismayed surprise: ". . . It is very ill, wonderfully ill . . so ill that I shut my eyes, & have the heartache . . only to think of it. So I will not. Why should we see things so differently, ever dearest? — If anyone had asked me, I could have answered for you that you saw it quite otherwise. And you would hang men even — you!"[5] Betty Miller, in her biography of Robert Browning, points out how Elizabeth expresses horror at Robert's belief in capital punishment and his relish in the thought of giving pain to an enemy. She sees his unquestioning acceptance of morally questionable customs as a relinquishment of personal conscience: "You are wrong . . when you advocate the pitiful resources of this corrupt social life."[6] Yet his greatest poem celebrates Pompilia Comparini *because* of her rejection of evil customs so strongly affirmed by society. Indeed, these words of Elizabeth Barrett could have been spoken by Pompilia to a Caponsacchi procrastinating in his resolve to rescue a wife from her husband because of the weight of custom. Even though Browning responds by return mail with a surprising admission of wrong for his pleasure in seeing an enemy "writhing with a sword thro' him up to the hilt,"[7] one hears its lingering echo in Caponsacchi's fantasizing of Guido's eternal punishment for his crimes against Pompilia (VI, 1905-54).

In the cultural fabric so meticulously delineated in *The Ring and the Book*, Browning shows how women are made use of to insure the maintenance of the patriarchal society. While he does not uphold the evils of patriarchy, his own relations with women are blatantly opportunistic. He uses women as comforters and bolsterers of his ego. His strong attachment to his mother is marked not only by filial devotion but by paralyzing dependence. As a young man he formed friendships with older women so there was no danger of romance or commitment. Nor did the ardor and loyalty that mark his male friendships have a parallel in his relations with women.[8] When he did marry the great love of his life, he burdened Elizabeth with the yoke of dominator which she did not wish to assume any more than he did himself. The invalided recluse with no worldly experience, who had been dominated by an overbearing father who had made all decisions for his captived children, was now given total responsibility for both their lives. She was to make all decisions while he sat at her feet in docile submission. After the bold rescue, Browning was helpless to make his way across France to Italy with his ailing and exhausted wife. In Paris, he placed himself under the protection of Anna Jameson, turning over to her the responsibility of getting them to Pisa. Before publishing *The Ring and the Book*, Browning shared the composition with Julia Wedgwood, whom he addressed in the endearing terms of friendship and trust until she showed irrevocable disagreement with and repugnance for his subject. One cringes at the poet's atrocious proposal to the elegant Lady Ashburton, assuring her that "the attractiveness of a marriage with her lay in its advantage to Pen."[9] In his last years Browning basked continuously and shamelessly in the adulation of rich ministering women.

Robert Browning shows himself as quite a conventional man when it comes to the issue of Elizabeth's association with George

Sand.[10] Though he went with his wife to pay calls on the novelist, he did so reluctantly, strongly disapproving the kind of society surrounding her. Is his fear of wifely contamination so different in its premise from Edward Moulton Barrett's paternal restraint? Elizabeth Barrett once had confided to Mary Russell Mitford that she would not tell her father about reading George Sand, far less seek his approval for her plan to actually contact her: "He has very strict ideas about women & about what they should read, . . and I heard him say once that he could not think highly of the modesty of any woman who could read Don Juan!!"[11] She goes on humorously to note his double standard, keeping for himself a canto of *Don Juan* "locked up from wandering eyes." Critics had chided Elizabeth Barrett as immodest for publishing poems praising Madame Dudevant: "George Sand: A Desire" and "To George Sand: A Recognition." John Kenyon reported to her that he had heard an "able man" say at his table: ". . . no modest woman would or *ought* to confess to an acquaintance with the works of George Sand."[12]

Many of the love letters carry on a lively argument over the French novelist — Elizabeth championing her as a great mind, great artist, and superior human being; Robert assessing her as undramatic and talkative, "*la femme qui parle.*"[13] To his credit, Robert Browning's side of the argument remains on artistic grounds, and he has no objection to what Elizabeth Barrett reads. Significant too is Browning's main objection to the content in Sand's *Consuelo*. In two different letters he complains about the protagonist's allowing herself to be bullied by a man. On 10 August 1845 he writes: "Who cares about Consuelo after that horrible evening with the Venetian scamp, (where he bullies her, and it does answer, after all she says) as we say?"[14] Five days later he elaborates on the same situation: "Then that horrible Porpora! — if George Sand gives *him* to a Consuelo for an absolute master, in consideration of his services specified, and . . . is of opinion that *they* warrant his conduct, or at least oblige submission to it, — then I find her objections to the fatherly rule of Frederic perfectly impertinent. . . ."[15] His reaction to this aspect of *Consuelo* is perfectly consistent with one of his major repugnances, tyranny. In January 1846[16] he tells Elizabeth about his recurring nightmares: "I stand by (powerless to interpose by word even) and see the infliction of tyranny on the unresisting. . . ." He then goes on to tell of an actual dinner party he attended where the host insulted his young wife, driving her from the room in tears and humiliation in order "to show off" before his dinner guests "(all males, law friends)." Browning is further incensed by the praise of a fellow guest for the host's possessing such a submissive, unprovoking wife. More revolting to him still is the sight of the subdued wife, dry-eyed and smiling meekly at her husband as she presided over his tea table after the incident. So strong was Browning's outrage that he broke completely with the unnamed host, and relates in a subsequent letter how the incident still haunts him.[17] This is very much the lover who wrote to Elizabeth Barrett concerning their future domestic relationship: ". . . I should never be able to say 'she shall dine on fish, on fruit,' 'She shall wear silk gloves or thread gloves' — even to exercise in fancy that much 'will *over* you' is revolting; I *will this*, never to be 'over you' if I could!"[18] This too is the rescuing lover who advised Elizabeth Barrett to leave a tyrannizing father. To submit to another's will, thereby relinquishing one's own, is, according to Robert Browning, to incur damnation: "All passive obedience and implicit submission of will and intellect is by far too easy, if well considered, to be the course prescribed by God to Man in this life of probation — for they *evade* probation altogether, tho' foolish people think otherwise: chop off your legs, you will never go astray — stifle your reason altogether and you will find it is difficult to reason ill: 'it is hard to make these sacrifices!' — Not so hard as to lose the reward or incur the penalty of an Eternity to come."[19] The domestic tyranny, which causes Browning the man such revulsion, affords Browning the poet grist for two of his most notable creations, the Duke of Ferrara and Count Guido

Franceschini. Even though, in the George Sand business, Browning himself manifests a sort of patriarchal protectionism in his reluctance to have his wife associate with a woman of notorious reputation, at least he does not implement it by exercising proprietorship over her choices and actions. He shows more consistency in this area than in others.

Knowledge of art and artists is one of Browning's richest resources in the making of poetry. Through his skillfully selective mining of painting and art history, the poet exposes the moral and psychological landscapes of some of his most memorable characters. Not only does he allow famous practitioners like Andrea del Sarto and Filippo Lippi to reveal their personalities through their respective styles of painting; he equally manifests the moral character of a collector like the Duke of Ferrara through the subjects he prefers. The poet of *The Ring and the Book* perceives, in the artistic tastes of Bottinius and Guido, a relish for the sexual exploitation of women. Both the prosecuting lawyer and the murdering spouse reveal their predatory sexual attitudes through their assessment of paintings, and their evaluations of live women by how they compare with particular artists' depictions of women subjects. Ironically, Browning has a strong personal predilection for the very type of painting he so ruthlessly exposes here, and the poet's defense of it takes some curious forms.

William De Vane[20] sees Browning's vituperative attack on the minor Florentine painter and critic, Filippo Baldinucci, culminating in his *Parleying with Francis Furini* (11. 144-73), as a defense, not only of Furini's female nudes, but of his artist son's as well. Browning is really attacking John Callcot Horsley, treasurer of the Royal Academy from 1882-97. Just as Baldinucci disapproved of Furini's female nudes as lascivious, so does Horsley judge Robert Widemann Browning's. The poet, who had suggested some of his son's subjects and treatments, and who wrote verses to accompany some of them, is defending his own taste as well as those of such painter friends as the prestigious Sir Frederic Leighton, who had a penchant for clothing his female subjects in transparent dresses. The vehemence of Browning's defense and his attribution of evil-in-the-eye-of-the-beholder to Furini's or Pen's critics is amazing in one who, from childhood through manhood, considered it the worst possible calamity to be seen himself in a state of undress. [21]

Browning's own favorite, "my Polidoro's perfect Andromeda" could most surely be the type the Fisc Bottinius relishes in his own word painting of female nudes in Book IX of *The Ring and the Book*. The painter of Browning's "Andromeda" is not the more famous Michelangelo Merisi da Caravaggio (c. 1565-1610), but the lesser known Polidoro Caldara (c. 1490-1543) known as Polidoro da Cara-vaggio. His "Andromeda," Mrs. Orr[22] tells us, was painted on a gar-den wall of the Palazzo del Bufalo in Rome and demolished sometime after Browning last saw it. An engraving of it, which the young poet kept over his desk for inspiration, resides in the British Museum. It was not among the memorabilia auctioned off in 1913 by the estate of Pen Browning. [23] Browning refers to the pictures in two early poems. In *Sordello* II the speaker compares the release of the poet's fancy to "Perseus when he loosed his naked love" (1.211). In the earlier *Pauline* (11. 656-77) he describes the subject in greater detail. The narrator, in a familiarly recurring fantasy, sees the sacrificial victim waiting for her loathsome devourer "quite naked and alone"; but the male viewer, while enjoying the prospect of her total female vulnerability, has no qualms because he knows for certain she will be rescued by "some god." That the viewer justifies himself indicates a certain unease at deriving aesthetic pleasure from the depiction of such a terrible im-molation. Perhaps Browning himself was aware of his own con-tradiction. At a later time he will use the woman-as-food metaphor to great effect in the mouth of Bottinius.

Elvan Kintner, in his introduction to the love letters, [24] cautions strongly against mythologizing the Barrett-Browning love story into Andromeda-Perseus, and with good reason. Elizabeth Barrett is no Andromeda. True, she was in a dreadful thralldom — 'the veriest slavery,"[25] as Browning called it—to Edward Moulton Barrett's paternal needs, and she never would have been delivered without Browning's persistence. In retrospect she saw clearly her tomb-like existence at Wimpole Street, but she never would have come to such clarity without him. Writing from Italy to her friend, Mrs. Martin, she reassesses her former state: "A thoroughly morbid and desolate state it was, which I look back on now with the sort of horror with which one would look to one's graveclothes, if one had been clothed in them by mistake during a trance."[26] Once he had helped her toward the act of will to escape, however, her "Red Cross Knight"[27] proved too incompetent to get an accurate train schedule to her for the dangerous exodus, and thereafter depended on his wife for all decision-making. Cinderella, as Elizabeth Barrett thought herself,[28] had somewhat of a pumpkin to deal with after she married her prince. Browning was no Perseus.

Flavia Alaya in her much praised essay, "The Ring, the Rescue & the *Risorgimento*,"[29] has pointed out Elizabeth Barrett Browning's radical revision of the crude material she inherited as a political metaphor for Italy: a victim, a woman, chained, despairing, with no inner potency, thus requiring an outside male rescuer—in short, an Andromeda. She saw how ill conceived such a metaphor would be for an oppressed but aspiring nation, or for her other great concern—the oppressed womanhood of nineteenth-century England. Elizabeth Barrett Browning transformed the archetypal rescue theme into a heroic mutual deliverance, reaching its most potent realization in *Aurora Leigh*. Alaya further points out how Elizabeth's material transformed the rescue theme so dear to her husband: "There could be no true heroism, finally, without the evocation of, and the acquiescence in, the heroism of others. Such an emphasis defines the most striking element of contrast between the 'obvious rescues' of Robert Browning's earlier poetry and the rescues of *The Ring and the Book*."[30] Pompilia is not Andromeda. If, as Dorothy Mermin has observed, the two poets write of the same kind of woman—not the helpless, passive woman celebrated by their contemporaries, but "women who have the courage to leave the position in which society confirms them"[31] — it is largely because Elizabeth Barrett Browning transformed the rescue myth from that of the helpless female delivered by the omnipotent male to a finite mutuality of deliverance. Pompilia rescues her two rescuers, Caponsacchi and Pope Innocent, who rightly see her as a hero. This is not the simplistic Andromeda-Perseus myth. In picture and in story Andromeda is always an object, never a hero. It is certain that the poet of *The Ring and the Book* does not see the Andromeda-Perseus myth in the same way as the poet of *Sordello* and *Pauline*.

The poet of *The Ring and the Book* is a feminist in ways strikingly at variance with some aspects of his puzzling life. If the pattern of his real life does not incarnate the subtlety, penetration, and consistency with which the poet of the Franceschini murder trial probes the warp and woof of patriarchy and its deleterious effect on women, so be it. I can only answer for the poem, not the enigmatic man. Elizabeth Barrett always had a problem reconciling the two Robert Brownings — the writer and the man. Readers of his poems, his letters, and his biographies are faced with the same problem, but is there a need to reconcile his personal contradictions in order to understand the poems? Let his own words to Elizabeth Barrett speak for him:

> Don't you remember I told you, once on a time, that you 'knew nothing of me'? whereat you demurred — but I meant what I said, & knew it was so. To be grand in a simile, for every poor speck of a Vesuvius or a Stromboli in my microcosm there are huge layers of ice and pits of black cold water — and I make the most of my two or three fire-eyes, because I know by experience, alas, how these tend to extinction — and the ice grows and grows — still this last is true part of me, most characteristic part, *best* part perhaps, and I disown nothing — only, when you talked of '*knowing* me'![32]

1 INTRODUCTION
THE FILTHY RAGS
OF SPEECH

. . . Learn one lesson hence
Of whatever lives should teach:
This lesson: that our human speech is nought,
Our human testimony false, our fame
And human estimation words and wind.
ROBERT BROWNING
The Ring and the Book
(XII, 832-6)

. . . Apart from my own incapacities of
whatever kind, I think this *is* the world as it is
and will be—*here* at least.
ROBERT BROWNING
to Julia Wedgwood

THE SEVENTEENTH-CENTURY Italian world of Robert Browning's *The Ring and the Book* abounds in, is leavened by, and exudes sexual cynicism. The notorious Roman murder trial of Count Guido Franceschini for the brutal slaying of his beautiful young runaway wife, Pompilia Comparini, is played against a background of public innuendo, mirth, sarcasm, or self-righteous indignation—all grounded in the traditional mores and attitudes of a patriarchal society, a culture suppressive of women. In such a culture, though a reverse grievance has no similar redress, a wife's adultery is just cause for her husband's execution of her. In this milieu, moreover, the husband's grievance is taken seriously and the wife accused of adultery is assumed guilty until proven innocent, if at all, after her death. What is extraordinary in this particular case is that Guido's plea of *honoris causa* is denied in spite of his sex and rank, and his wife's conduct eventually exonerated in spite of hers.

The circumstances leading to the actual trial are prime for rampant gossip and innuendo: a young wife runs away from her nobleman husband in the company of a handsome young society-priest; the angry husband with his retainers overtakes the renegade pair at Castelnuovo en route to Rome from Arezzo; at the consequent trial, amid much mirth and snickering, the ecclesiastical court relegates the priest to three years' banishment in the remote Civita Vecchia and the pregnant wife to the Scalette Convent for her confinement. Then, a year later, the husband's wrath belatedly comes to fruition. With the assistance of four hired assassins, he surprises the Comparini family one night during Christmastide, and violently slays the young mother and her parents in their home. The newly born son, away nursing, was spared capture. Had it ended there, all might have been well for the outraged husband. But Guido and his men are overtaken before reaching the security of their own Tuscany, and Pompilia lives on for four days to tell her own story, exonerating from her deathbed herself and her rescuer Giuseppe Maria Caponsacchi, former canon at the Pieve. The court believes her this time and sentences her murderers to death.

To say that Pompilia's conduct would be unacceptable in the Italy of 1697 would be an understatement. But even more intriguing is that such conduct was so efficaciously thinkable in the character created by Browning. That a docile, passive, seventeen-year-old girl, married four years to a worldly aristocrat three times her age, would firmly resolve to run away from her husband; to make the decision in total isolation, without parental advice; to go directly contrary to counsel sought from the highest civil and ecclesiastical authority available; to take such a resolve with absolutely no means to carry it out; to brave the opprobrium of all society and incur the wrath of a violent vindictive husband; and to do it all in the face of an enlightened personal fear — all this is a measure of Pompilia's courage, self-possession, self-direction, and sense of sole responsibility for the preservation of self. For such an inexperienced girl to take such resolve and unflinchingly implement it in the face of such odds is remarkable. And indeed Browning has created a remarkable young woman in the *persona* of his Pompilia Comparini. For what provokes her radical behavior is an even more radical judgment: that her husband's sexual treatment of her was a degradation inimical to the point of perdition through either corruption or despair. It is a judgment against culture, going counter to a basic and deeply rooted myth to which she will not assent: that woman is created to pleasure man; that a wife is a possession to be disposed with as her husband sees fit. She is instructed very bluntly in her marital duties not only by her husband, but by the archbishop and the governor as well, and the youthful Pompilia rejects all their counsel. Mild and passive though she is, Pompilia stands as Yeats' stone in the living stream, dividing the waters, disturbing the flow, of custom, of thought, of the culture itself. Like Antigone, her self-direction puts her in opposition to society's values manifested in power. The poet-novelist created a character of unusual stature and great spiritual power. Pompilia, not Guido, is the moral focus of the drama. Guido, after all, does nothing contrary to the culture—a point he reiterates constantly in his defense. It is Pompilia who is on trial for her decisions and values which go contrary to cultural mores. The final judgment of the court on her behalf is a moral victory for her and a reversal of societal norms.

Guido's act of murder was never in question—only whether he was justified in its execution. Defense of a husband's honor was legitimate cause for murdering a wife. His waiting a year to execute his wrath undoubtedly vitiated Guido's plea of outraged honor, but, in the end, the nobleman of Arezzo was sentenced to death for the triple murder only because the court judged Pompilia innocent of adultery. The whole proceeding—the defense, the prosecution, the verdict—was based upon this question on the title page of what Browning called the Old Yellow Book:[1] ". . . Whether and when a Husband may kill his Adulterous Wife. . . ." The vested curiosity and the popular verdicts, however, assumed her guilt. Exoneration of Pompilia, guilty or not, would establish a dangerous precedent and raise a troublesome question in a society whose main prop was the "Supremacy of husband over wife" (X, 2034). The sentencing of the Count would dilute the principle of *honoris causa* upon which society was based. The case, accordingly, was a *cause célèbre* evoking opinions from everyone. Browning's reconstructions of these public opinions are fraught with the errors of human bias, selective perception, moral incompetence, culpable ignorance, and self-interest. Each contemporary version of the facts is clothed in what Browning calls the "filthy rags of speech" (X, 372).

The case in court is a confessed murder. The screams of the victims enabled neighbors to alert the authorities who caught the culprits literally red-handed before they left Rome. Yet, in the world Browning has resuscitated, one would think Pompilia the defendant. As is common in crimes of violence against women, the victim is the focus of popular and ecclesiastical judgment: Did she bring this fate upon herself by her own sin and provocation? Upon her actions and character speculation feeds and swells. Not until Book VII does she speak for herself, tell her own version of events. By the time she gets to speak on her own behalf, she has been condemned roundly. Guido's "Half-Rome"—the half that sides with the cause of husband's honor—considers the dying girl of no consequence, "this poor gilded fly Pompilia-thing" (II, 1356). He sees her in the traditional role of a lamia: ". . . the snake / Pompilia writhed transfixed through all her spires" (II, 794-5). To him Guido is a hero preserving and restoring order and civilization. Indeed, he should have, Rolando-like "Slain the priest gallant and wife-paramour" (II, 1497) the year before. The two culprits are Eve and Lucifer forever plotting the downfall of Edenic man. He even discredits, before we can hear Caponsacchi's defense of Pompilia in Book VI, the priest's testimony as a story to regale a saloon during Carnival (II, 1453).

"The Other Half-Rome" advocates the young wife, but his testimony is fuzzy-minded and sentimental. With superb illogic he exonerates Pompilia while finding Caponsacchi guilty:

> We deal here with no innocent at least,
> No witless victim,—he's a man of age
> And a priest beside,—persuade the mocking world
> Mere charity boiled over in this sort!
> (III, 816-19)

Such advocacy is damning, and Pompilia, no matter how sympathetically portrayed by such a double tongue, comes out an adulterer. The urbane "Tertium Quid" sees the whole thing, not as tragedy, but farce. With lurid imagination he reconstructs the grisly murders on which his final judgment is that Guido acted within his rights as husband, and should be treated with leniency because "He is noble, and he may be innocent" (III, 1624). "Tertium Quid" is the quintessential snob who keeps the proper distance of objectivity, the detached observer, the "understander of the mind of man" (III, 61), supposedly withholding judgment while suffusing all testimony with sarcasm. Of course, of all the preliminary speakers, the greatest debasement of Pompilia's character comes from Guido (Book IV) who will get yet another opportunity to speak in the penultimate book of Browning's poem. He indeed has the last word. To him Pompilia is "the mongrel of a drab," a "mongrel-brat," his chattel. Killing her was his right and duty. He confidently bids the court, "Absolve, then, me, law's mere executant!" (IV, 2003).

The ten inner monologues comprising the verse-novel[2] proper are heavily weighted against Pompilia. All the speakers except herself are, significantly, men representing a patriarchal society to whom her conduct is deviant, thereby making her, *ipso facto*, guilty till proven innocent. Only two of them believe in her innocence and unequivocally declare it — Caponsacchi (Book VI) and the Pope (Book X), and the former is, as a principal, under a cloud of sexual innuendo. All the rest, except The Other Half-Rome, are sympathetic to the murderer who, in his turn, gets to speak twice. Even Pompilia's lawyer, Bottinius, believes her guilty, defending her only by the cynical weapon of casuistry. In *The Ring and the Book*, the victim is on trial by a populace represented, in turn by legal systems — secular and ecclesiastical — inimical to the disruption of the *status quo*. All are weighers of evidence, examining more or less carefully the verifiable facts. They do not draw the same conclusions. For each one the truth is alloyed with the self—its biases, inclinations, and experiences. Though the problem of appearance versus reality is a universal theme in literature and the basis of all tragic irony, nowhere more than in *The Ring and the Book* is there such a focus on human fallibility in the interpretation of incontrovertible facts—what most people would concede to be reality itself. How Browning manages such a maze is astounding.[3] How, out of such "filthy rags of speech," he can manage to clothe Pompilia in the white garment of truth is a consummate feat of craftsmanship. For in the poem Pompilia Comparini comes through as nonpareil, "earth's flower" (X, 107), "Perfect in whiteness" (X, 1005).

When on "that remarkable day" (I, 91), a June day in 1860, Robert Browning picked up for a lira in the Piazza di San Lorenzo, Florence, an old yellowed book, a collection of documents concerning a Roman murder trial of 1698, he knew he had discovered something remarkable, something particularly akin to his brand of creativity. By the time he reached home at Casa Guidi across the Arno, he ". . . had mastered the contents, knew the whole truth / Gathered together, bound up in this book" (I, 117-8). But what is the *truth* Browning saw? ". . . In this book lay absolute truth, / Fanciless fact," he firmly believed. Since the documents were full of conflicting points of view, and the poet was anything but simple-minded, he saw his creative task to extract from a maze of contradictions the true characters and motives of the principals involved in this domestic murder case.

From the obsessive initial reading Browning turned "to free" himself "and find the world" (I, 478). But as he looked from his narrow terrace over the familiar sights of the darkened streets of Florence, his inward eye was already moving again toward Arezzo which he saw as "the man's town, / The woman's trap and cage and torture-place" (I, 501-2). His judgment is already formed. Indeed, he recounts how he reconstructed the whole story buried in the facts of the Old Yellow Book, churning it into immediate drama with living characters enacting and reenacting the various scenes of Pompilia's life, beginning and ending tragically in Rome. The details of physical description become pointedly concrete and quite significant as embodiments of spiritual reality. All the characters eventually emerge full-blown from the forge of the poet.

In their greedy and foolish haste to procure an aristocratic husband for their daughter, the Comparini go scrambling through "The world's mud, careless if it splashed and spoiled" (I, 551). Guido, their prize, the poet conceives as ". . . the star supposed, but fog o' the fen, / Guilded star-fashion by a glint of hell" (I, 544-5). Guido's two priest brothers, Abate Paolo and Canon Girolamo, take shape as

> Two obscure goblin creatures, fox face this,
> Cat-clawed the other . . . cloaked and caped,
> Making as they were priests, to mock God more.
> (I, 549-52)

These brothers, as marriage-brokers, become

> These who rolled the starlike pest to Rome
> And stationed it to suck up and absorb
> The sweetness of Pompilia, rolled again
> That bloated bubble, with her soul inside,
> Back to Arezzo and a palace there.
> (554-8)

The image of Count Guido as an ingurgitating bubble swallowing up Pompilia's soul is a terrifying variation of St. George's original dragon. It is like an assimilating amoeba, feeding its own substance with its captive's self. The Franceschini are a "satyr-family" (570); the mother, "a grey mother with a monkey-mien / Mopping and mowing. . . ." (571-2). Browning perceives Pompilia's situation, when abandoned by her parents in the house of the Franceschini, as both murderous and perditious:

> These I saw
> In recrudescency of baffled hate,
> Prepare to wring the uttermost revenge
> From body and soul thus left them: all was sure,
> Fire laid and cauldron set, the obscene ring traced,
> The victim stripped and prostrate. . . .
> (577-82)

Into this scene "sprang the young good beauteous priest" (586), Giuseppe Maria Caponsacchi, "in a glory of armor like Saint George" (585), who saved Pompilia for "a splendid minute" from Arezzo to Castelnuovo before Guido's overtaking them "once more canopied the world with black" (602).

In his preliminary explanations of method in Book I, Browning alternates between the development of his gold-alloy metaphor and the actual fleshing out of his characters and scenes from the raw material of the law documents.[4] His method of characterization is a verbal demonstration of the methods of goldcraft. Each time he returns to develop his *personae*, the poet engages in a more specific delineation, going from appearance, to gesture, to speech, to motive—from outer to inner landscape. The motion of creation is like a spiral, a spring gathering more force of definition as it proceeds. What Browning read in the turgid law-Latin of the Old Yellow Book his incandescent mind crafted into these living, motivated people. To him, "in this book lay absolutely truth" (143). To dig out the "lingot truth" from the bare facts was his task. This is crucial to Browning. His ring metaphor is the way he selected to explain how he approaches truth through art. The poem is, after all, a creature of art; it has a life of its own wrought by the poet from the raw material of his source: "I fused my live soul with this inert stuff, / Before attempting smithcraft. . . ." (469-70). To Browning, here and elsewhere, his avowed path to truth is through art. That is the only way for him. Nor does he confuse the two. Browning's is the artistic voice that knows the limitations of human speech—his own included. He is also the poet who celebrates all human limitations as the stuff of human hope. He knows the elusiveness of truth—how difficult to apprehend with the finite intelligence further restrained by its own cultivation—yet he faces these limitations and plunges ahead, not shrinking from his resources of judgment and creativity. He invites the reader to do the same, exert judgment:

> . . . See it for yourselves,
> This man's act, changeable because alive!
> Action now shrouds, now shows the informing thought;
> Man, like a glass ball with a spark a-top,
> Out of the magic fire that lurks inside,
> Shows one tint at a time to take the eye:
> Which, let a finger touch the silent sleep,
> Shifted a hair's-breadth shoots you dark for bright,
> Suffuses bright with dark, and baffles so
> Your sentence absolute for shine or shade.
> (1364-73)

With his Pope Innocent, Browning, in contemplating the documents of the trial, knows that

> Truth, nowhere, lies yet everywhere in these—
> Not absolutely in a portion, yet
> Evolvable from the whole. . . .
> (x, 228-30)

Evolvable is a crucial word here, entirely appropriate to the process by which Browning has given life to his characters. And, like some of his other recreations, Abt Vogler and Fra Filippo Lippi, Browning can only infer the truth through contemplation of reality as observed and interpreted through his own limited facilities; and, like them, he can convey it only through his art:

> Why take the artistic way to prove so much?
> Because it is the glory and good of Art,
> That Art remains the only way possible
> Of speaking truth, to mouths like mine, at least.
> (XII, 837-40)

The truth Browning strives for in his resuscitation of the Roman murder case is the truth of the human heart in conflict. The world of man we see in this poem is evil; the darkness of the human heart seems to prevail:

> A faultless creature is destroyed, and sin
> Has had its way i' the world where God should rule.
> (X, 1420-1)

When Julia Wedgwood objected to the overpowering evil in *The Ring and the Book*, Browning defended his vision: "Apart from my own incapacities of whatever kind, I think this *is* the world as it is and will be—*here* at least."[5] Unlike Julia Wedgwood, however, many readers have no problem recognizing the verisimilitude of evil in Browning's poem; the problem is the poet's presentation of goodness. Evil is accepted as a given; goodness is not. Consequently the ring metaphor is considered false.

The English public in 1868-9 received Browning's masterpiece with unexpected enthusiasm,[6] but the oracular dissenting voice of Thomas Carlyle summarily dismissed the whole endeavor of his literary colleague as based on an absurdity—the possibility of love between woman and man to be other than genital: "But the whole is on the most absurd basis. The real story is plain enough in looking into it; the girl and the handsome young priest were lovers."[7] This voice has been heard to this day and, most likely, will always be. The voices Browning invented to give substance to contemporary reactions to the sordid murder trial of 1698 are, interestingly, the voices and opinions running as a carping strain through reactions of a number of readers who simply cannot accept Browning's characterization of two principals—Pompilia Comparini and Giuseppe Caponsacchi. Given the facts, these readers cannot believe in the innocence of the runaway wife and her priest rescuer, anymore than could the speakers of the Roman populace in Browning's work. The persisting, continually recurring resistance to the poet's ring metaphor is perhaps underlain, in many cases, by deep-seated rejection of his very characterizations themselves. This resistance, if not outright rejection, seems rooted in a strong sexual cynicism—a suspicion in some readers that Browning could not have created these people as they actually were: the *facts* would have to dictate otherwise. In such readers sexual skepticism, not historical curiosity, motivates the itch to get behind Browning's interpretation—considered a deliberate illusion—and find out what *really* happened, and, it would seem, rewrite the novel for him. This frame of mind finds it impossible to afford Robert Browning a poetic faith in his characterization of Pompilia Comparini, the characterization central to the moral focus of his reconstruction of the Franceschini murder story. The love between Pompilia and Caponsacchi seems to be beyond their human comprehension and certainly beyond belief: a love between a woman and a man not ending in sexual consummation. Unlike the Pope, who found it "easy to believe" in the purity of the wife and the priest "in thought, word and deed" (X, 1170), they cannot accept such a love.

The desire to investigate the intriguing history of the period of a great work of art, particularly a dramatic one, is natural and will always engage the minds of readers and literary historians. Browning's rejuvenation of a little-known period of Italian history, his focus upon real people in an actual murder trial, his particular fleshing out of characters who hardly exist dimensionally in the documents of the Old Yellow Book and his other source[8] naturally make readers want to know more. Shakespeare's history plays have sent unlikely readers to Plutarch's *Lives*. Browning's dramatic monologues have sent readers into investigations of the House of Este, the painting

are, in Browning's own words, "such inert stuff," a reader would be compelled to do something. The end result would be, if not so brilliant as Browning's, at least as much of a mixture of imagination and fact as to resemble the process of smithcraft, the poet's chosen metaphor.

The purpose of this study is not to reject Robert Browning's method of creation as symbolized by the ring metaphor, nor to reject the resulting characterization inspired by his reading of source material. Nor is it to reconstruct the facts from sources since brought to light by literary historians roused by the human fascination of Robert Browning's murder story.[10] The purpose is to examine the drama of Pompilia as Browning created her: the explicitly sexual degradation by Guido and his priest brother; the clear-headed judgment of her situation and the remarkable self-direction in one so young and docile in spite of all authority, civil and ecclesiastical; the surpassing lyricism, gaiety, and *caritas* of the love between her and Caponsacchi. Browning has, in his reconstruction of the facts as he culled them from his sources, created a surpassing love story, original and provocative— one having the power to stand our culture's more jaded conception of sexual love on its head, and strike readers with awe. The love of Pompilia and Caponsacchi is one of the great love stories of all time, and, *because* it is neither adulterous nor sacrilegious, it restores to the reader's contemplation some of the mystery of sexual love not often brought to the reader's attention in current literature.

and characters of Fra Filippo Lippi and Andrea del Sarto recorded in Vasari's *Lives of the Artists*. He did, after all, write of real traceable historical figures who existed in specific times and places. Dramatic figures of history always have engaged creative artists, and any perusal of painting and literature manifests how much each artist's conception of a given figure can differ from another's. Jean Anouilh and George Bernard Shaw have created two different characterizations of the historical Joan of Arc in their respective plays, *The Lark* and *Saint Joan*, and Shakespeare makes her a prostitute. These recreated historical figures are *personae*. Variant, even contradictory, characterizations can emerge in divers artists' minds from contemplation of the same facts. We do not accuse these playwrights of dishonesty. Instead, we afford them poetic faith, accepting their characterizations within the worlds of their respective plays, even when we disagree with their historicity. We are able to distinguish between historical persons and *dramatis personae*. Perhaps the more famous and established in human consciousness the subject is, the more we allow the artist to reinvent the personality from the facts.

Browning perhaps suffers in this particular work because, until he wrote *The Ring and the Book*, no one in the English-speaking world ever had heard of Count Guido Franceschini and Pompilia Comparini and the once notorious trial. Then too, the work is of such enormous volume and so narrow a scope—the same story told over and over by different characters—that Browning had almost unlimited possibilities to develop *personae* commensurate with such a horrifying situation and actions. Because the poet's main source, the Old Yellow Book, became available for others to investigate the facts of the case, it stands to reason that other interpreters might produce in their own imagination characters of a different complexion with variant motivations. The point is that readers examining the Browning source material for themselves would use their imagination to flesh out the characters involved in such dramatic action.[9] Because the documents themselves readers who simply cannot accept Browning's characterization of two principals—Pompilia Comparini and Giuseppe Caponsacchi. Given the facts, these readers cannot believe in the innocence of the runaway wife and her priest rescuer, anymore than could the speakers of the Roman populace in Browning's work. The persisting, continually recurring resistance to the poet's ring metaphor is perhaps underlain, in many cases, by deep-seated rejection of his very characterizations themselves. This resistance, if not outright rejection, seems rooted in a strong sexual cynicism—a suspicion in some readers that Browning could not have created these people as they actually were: the *facts* would have to dictate otherwise. In such readers sexual skepticism, not historical curiosity, motivates the itch to get behind Browning's interpretation—considered a deliberate illusion—and find out what *really* happened, and, it would seem, rewrite the novel for him. This frame of mind finds it impossible to afford Robert Browning a poetic faith in his characterization of Pompilia Comparini, the characterization central to the moral focus of his reconstruction of the Franceschini murder story. The love between Pompilia and Caponsacchi seems to be beyond their human comprehension and certainly beyond belief: a love between a woman and a man not ending in sexual consummation. Unlike the Pope, who found it "easy to believe" in the purity of the wife and the priest "in thought, word and deed" (X, 1170), they cannot accept such a love.

The desire to investigate the intriguing history of the period of a great work of art, particularly a dramatic one, is natural and will always engage the minds of readers and literary historians. Browning's rejuvenation of a little-known period of Italian history, his focus upon real people in an actual murder trial, his particular fleshing out of characters who hardly exist dimensionally in the documents of the Old Yellow Book and his other source[8] naturally make readers want to know more. Shakespeare's history plays have sent unlikely readers to Plutarch's *Lives*. Browning's dramatic monologues have sent readers into investigations of the House of Este, the painting

2 *HONORIS CAUSA*: MISOGYNY IN CHURCH AND SOCIETY

. . . In this case the spirit and culture speaks,
Civilization is imperative. . . .
The Ring and the Book
. (X, 2016-7)

                                    Take
Count Guido's life, and sap society,
Whereof the main prop was, is, and shall prove
—Supremacy of husband over wife.
(X, 2031-4)

                              . . . Rascality
Enlisted, rampant on the side of hearth
Home and the husband. . . .
(VI, 1537-9)

. . . Where's the bond obliges horse to man
Like that which binds fast wife to husband?
(XI, 1400-1)

Guido's Defense

GUIDO'S MARRIAGE to Pompilia was a mismatch by age, class, education, and temperament. The disparity, however, runs much deeper than any of these elements. We learn, in the process of understanding the two persons, that the rift between them is a disparity in the very quality of their souls. As this disparity becomes manifest through their respective monologues, we see it as the source of Guido's surpassing hatred and mysterious malevolence toward his wife. The public, however, seems uninterested in the mysterious subtleties of this couple's spiritual drama. Though Count Guido Franceschini is on trial for murder, the issue is the virtue of his victim. Pompilia Comparini is on trial as an erring wife, a violator of husbandly honor. Because Guido's spiritual quality is reflected in society, that society has no problem supporting him in his defense of such an overt, cowardly, and heinous crime. The sympathetic bond between the nobleman and his auditors is the base for his brash, swaggering bravado about the murder by himself and four armed men of an old man, an old woman, and a seventeen-year-old girl recovering from childbirth. Hardly the stuff of heroism, yet Guido speaks from an eminence of security with the swagger of cheap heroics.

The marriage was founded on greed — a tradeoff of money for prestige, with the bridled girl as the gilded prize. Count Franceschini admits to buying his wife as one buys an ox or ass or chattel; he forestalls public criticism:

'What?
No blush at the avowal you dared buy
A girl of age beseems your granddaughter,
Like ox or ass? Are flesh and blood a ware?
Are heart and soul a chattel?'
(V, 426-30)

Guido affirms his wife's heart and soul are just that, and his meto-
nymic method of defining his possession is fit language for his attitude. He is irked that Pompilia refuses to participate in the pact, that
she cannot see herself as chattel. He calls upon the law to vindicate his
claim:

. . . The law's the law:
With a wife I look to find all wifeliness
As when I buy, timber and twig, a tree—
I buy the song 'o the nightingale inside.

Such was the pact: Pompilia from the first
Broke it, refused from the beginning day
Either in body or soul to cleave to mine. . . .
(v, 603-10)

He is not even touching on her alleged adultery here, but on her lack
of connubial cooperation. At first this might seem a just grievance,
except that his language betrays him, giving us a hint of what he expected from his purchased chattel. Over and over he iterates that
Pompilia is his possession, body and soul. He says she is

. . . a hawk
I bought at hawk's price and carried home
To do hawk's service. . . .
(v, 703-5)

Guido's language, as he gets into stride, gains in crudeness. Blatantly, he states that his wife has no right to his love. His and his wife's respective marital roles are bluntly spelled out:

> The obligation I incurred was just
> To practise mastery, prove my mastership: —
> Pompilia's duty was — submit herself,
> Afford me pleasure, perhaps cure my bile.
> (v, 716-9)

To get his "penny's worth" from his purchase, he will

> . . . hoodwink, starve and properly train my bird,
> And, should she prove a haggard, — twist her neck!
> (v, 709-10)

Guido's language is hardly edifying, nor does he bother to make it so. Its tone of familiarity indicates his cool assumption that his audience of jurors concurs with his own values. They are one; he speaks for society. Thus, his admission that he took a foolish course in not punishing Pompilia early on for displeasing him. If he had "with the vulgarest household implement, / Calmly and quietly cut off, clean thro' the bone, / But one joint of the finger" (V, 952-4) of his wife, this action would have been considered "the natural vengeance" (V, 1070), moderate, wise, and appropriate to stem a wife's evil inclinations and prevent her provoking eventual and inevitable death at the hands of an irked husband. He admits he was remiss in prevention, but sees his eventual killing of Pompilia as a release, a cure, the lancing of an ulcer allowed to grow untended. In murdering his wife and her parents, Guido asserts with utmost confidence of sympathetic understanding: "I did / God's bidding and man's duty, so, breathe free" (V, 1702-3). It is as if he, by his triple murder, administered sacramental absolution to himself for culpable negligence of manly duty in not having tended the problem sooner. Pompilia, after all, in the previous trial, was found guilty of adultery, and would have been sentenced to life imprisonment by Tuscan law, if not Roman. Thus Guido can address the court with confidence: "The wife, you allow so far, I have not wronged" (V, 1869). The law agreed that Guido's marital treatment of his wife was blameless. And to have killed Pompilia and Capon-sacchi at Castelnuovo, on the spot, at the time of her flight would have been "the license law's self gives" (V, 1878). No matter that they are subsequently proved innocent. In pleading his case before this tribunal, Guido's rhetoric rises to a crescendo in a visionary patriotic encomium of the new Rome, a Utopia to be brought about by the court's "brave decision" to absolve him as the "law's executant" (V, 2003). Rhapsodically he defines Rome as a place restored by brave deeds such as his murders:

> Husbands once more God's representatives,
> Wives like the typical Spouse once more. . . .
> (V, 2043-4)

By "typical Spouse," Guido means all those things implied by his language and tone—a wife submissive to her husband's will in all things.

In the midst of Guido's lecture on the meaning of marriage he chides his listeners in the governor's court:

> Am I to teach my lords what marriage means,
> What God ordains thereby and man fulfills? . . .
> (V, 720-1)

It would not seem to be necessary, considering what we hear voiced by other members of society in the various monologues. These voices all emerge from a long-lived, well-preserved, sacredly guarded tradition of patriarchy.

Secular Authority

In Book I the poet goes through a list of case histories, actually entered among the documents of the Franceschini case, recording morally justified precedents for wife-killing. With mock erudition he recounts "A true tale which has edified each child" schooled in the tradition of his fathers. From Claudius Aeleanus's *Variae Historiae, On the Nature of Animals* Browning selects the story

> Of the elephant who, brute-beast though he were,
> Yet understood and punished on the spot
> His master's naughty spouse and faithless friend.
> (I, 234-6)

The irony is Browning's, for such evidence indeed was entered seriously into the documents of moral and legal defense for Count Franceschini. The poet expends much mirth noting celebrated authorities: Solon and his Athenians, the code of Romulus and Rome, Justinian, Cornelia de Sicariis, Pompeia de Parricidiis, the Lex Julia, King Solomon, the Apostle Paul, and more. The various testimonies in the Old Yellow Book

> . . . heaped themselves
> From earth's four corners, all authority
> And precedent for putting wives to death,
> Or letting wives live, sinful though they seem.
> (I, 217-20)

The point of all these documents is the subjugation of woman based on her innate inferiority and consequent inclination to evil. As Aristotle established long before: "We should look upon the female state as being as it were a deformity, though one which occurs in the ordinary course of nature."[1] Aristotle realizes women are indispensable to generating the species. Patriarchal Rome follows antiquity, and Christianity follows both of these while adhering to Judaic tradition concerning women. Indeed, the whole Graeco-Roman / Judeo-Christian tradition is represented in the selected authorities cited in the Franceschini murder case.

It would be enlightening to sample some of these and other documents representing the sum of secular authority from which seventeenth-century Rome was formed. What were their respective contributions to the legal disposition of women in their various societies? From the poet Philomen we learn that "it was Solon who, because of young men's unbridled passions, first made a law whereby women might be prostituted in brothels."[2] To Romulus, the legendary founder of Rome (753 B. C.), is credited the first law concerning marriage. From various accounts we learn different aspects of the Code of Romulus as they are cited in the Old Yellow Book of the Franceschini trial. From Dionysius of Halicarnassus we are told that "This law obliged . . . the married women, as having no other refuge, to conform themselves entirely to the temper of their husbands and the husbands to rule their wives as necessary and inseparable possessions. . . ."[3] Romulus permitted the husband and his relations to punish an adulterous wife by death. Following the accepted practice and emphasizing the double standard of the law, the authority of the illustrious Marcus Cato (232-147 B. C.) is cited three centuries after his death:

> I have copied Marcus Cato's words from the oration entitled *On the Dowry*, in which it is also stated that husbands had the right to kill wives taken in adultery. . . . Further, as to the right to put her to death, it was thus written: 'If you should take your wife in adultery, you may with impunity put her to death without trial; but if you should commit adultery or indecency, she must not presume to lay a finger on you, nor does the law allow it.'[4]

Again, in regard to adultery, *The Code of Justinian* cites the *Lex Julia* — both of these codes were used as authorities in the Franceschini case: "The *Lex Julia* declares that wives have no right to bring criminal accusations for adultery against their husbands, . . . for while the law grants this privilege to men it does not concede it to women."[5]

Livy, in his *History of Rome*, cites Marcus Porcius Cato on the

nature of women and the concomitant necessity for men to keep
them in tow:

> Woman is a violent and uncontrolled animal, and it is useless to
> let go the reins and then expect her not to kick over the traces.
> You must keep her on a tight rein. . . . Women want total
> freedom or rather—to call things by their names—total licence.
> If you allow them to achieve complete equality with men, do
> you think they will be easier to live with? Not at all. Once they
> have achieved equality, they will be your masters.[6]

This sentiment is repeated over and over. In *The Institutes of Gaius* we
read that "the ancients required women, even if they were of full age,
to remain under guardianship on account of the levity of their disposition."[7] And one sees this assessment of woman's character in the many
handbooks of correct conduct for secular gentlemen with which the
social history of Italy abounds. In his *Handbook of Good Customs*, Paola
da Certaldo, a Florentine businessman, wrote: "The female is an
empty thing and easily swayed: she runs great risks when she is away
from her husband. Therefore, keep females in the house, keep them as
close to yourselves as you can, and come home often to keep an eye on
your affairs and to keep them in fear and trembling."[8] Guido perfectly
exemplified such an attitude three hundred years after the publication
of this conduct book of a fellow Tuscan.

These are examples of the time-honored authorities of the Rome of
the Franceschini trial. It is from such a background and such bonded
assurance that Guido speaks in his own defense. He has solid expectations from the secular powers trying his case. But what of the spiritual
authorities? What could he expect from the church?

Ecclesiastical Authority

The gross materialism of the ecclesiastical quarter seems even more cynical than that of its secular counterpart. Women are used as commodities of exchange for higher investiture of power. Guido's brother, Abate Paolo, in arranging the ill-starred marriage between Pompilia and the Count, quips that "Mothers, wives, and maids / These be the tools wherewith priests manage men" (IV, 501-2). Each category of woman is a tool, a means of one group of men, the clergy, to manipulate and control another, the laity. Power is the prime value of this society, and the men on top represent a church whose values and activities are centered in and motivated by the desire to dominate. As "princes of the church" the hierarchy must lord it over the laymen, including the aristocracy. According to Paolo Franceschini, the chief means of managing this pyramid is women, to be pawned by the clergy as prizes, rewards to material loyalty in conduct and reciprocal favor.

Caponsacchi had been caught up in this during his first assignment as a society priest whose role was to entertain rich and influential women — influential because they had been placed by the hierarchy in marriages arranged and implemented with clerical mediation. The chain of influence thus established would pay off with interest if properly maintained. After his conversion Caponsacchi analyzes the ecclesiastical chess game as a system devised to insure the established order vested in patriarchy, whether clerical or lay. Maintenance was based in cynicism, providing wealthy women with a kind of clerical *cavaliere servente*. The security of the system required the marketing of women. Rich women were allowed their flirtations with young priests to keep their homes intact. These flirtations could be controlled by the ecclesiastical court, kept within the clerical body which no secular power could touch. The privileged woman was kept happy and occupied while her husband was following the double standard of extra-marital relations completely acceptable to the clergy. Thus the home and hearth were maintained with the aid of clerical cynicism.

Pompilia's marriage did not fit into all this for three reasons: her husband, a ruined aristocrat, was a miser and kept his wife in poverty; a jealous spouse, he kept her sequestered from the world; and Pompilia, true to self, was uninclined—in or out of marriage—to pursuits of unchastity as a means of diversion or recreation. Guido, moreover, indulged his sense of power by keeping his wife in a state of fear and exercising cruelty over her—a perfect exemplar of the metaphysics of pornography. Yet Guido undeviatingly claims he is in his behavior a loyal son of the church and an exemplary representative of society. And he is right: the church concurred that established and approved society consisted of men and of men's women whose role was to be silent and to cooperate, to see that men's wishes were fulfilled always.

The church's magisterial tradition stands firmly behind the suppression of women, basing its theory and practice of misogyny in scripture and tradition as a direct mandate from God. Before going into the particulars of Guido's treatment of his wife and the solid backing it found from the church, it would be well to review some salient attitudes of notable clerics toward women. The shocking misogyny in the evolution of Christian theology has an early spokesman in St. Paul's[9] famous instruction: "The head of the woman is the man. . . . For a man indeed ought not to cover his head, forasmuch as he is the image and glory of God: but the woman is the glory of the man. For the man is not of the woman; but the woman of the man. Neither was the man created for the woman; but the woman for the man" (I Corinthians 11:7-9). The last line could be used, unaltered, as a statement of editorial policy for a pornographic publication. In the same epistle Paul exhorts, "Let your women keep silence in the churches: for it is not permitted unto them to speak; but they are commanded to be under obedience. . . . And if they will learn anything, let them ask their husbands at home: for it is a shame for a woman to speak in the church" (I Cor. 14:34-5). It is difficult to reconcile these passages with the celebrated hymn on *caritas* which comes between them in chapter 13 of First Corinthians. Nor is it easy to see how such statements coexist in the Apostle's mind with such pronouncements as, "There is neither Jew nor Greek, there is neither bond nor free, there is neither male nor female: for you are all one in Christ Jesus" (Galatians 3:28). Paul has, of course, inherited the tradition of Jewish misogyny, lethally combining it with that of Graeco-Roman culture for further authority. What was put forth so emphatically in the *Genesis* myth of the Fall, Paul feels compelled to explicate and expound upon with greater emphasis on the evil of womankind: "I suffer not a woman to teach, nor to usurp authority over the man, but to be in silence. For Adam was first formed, then Eve. And Adam was not deceived, but the woman being deceived was in the transgression: (I Timothy 2:12-4). *Genesis* makes the woman responsible for the fall of man and makes woman second in the order of creation. The generation of life is attributed by the author of *Genesis* only to man: from the rib of the wombless Adam Eve is produced. From then on, it is her function to produce new life, but it was imperative for the hierarchical order of patriarchy to have her emanate from the body of Adam. Although the *Genesis* account of the creation states that "In the image of God, he created them. Male and female he created them" (I, 34), it is obvious from the grammar who is made more in God's image. From the dual authorities of *Genesis* and Paul the Christian tradition produced a formidable line of theologians reiterating the evils of women, thereby developing the separate definition of woman as outside the image of God.

From St. John Chrysostom we are told "The woman taught, once and ruined all. . . . The sex is weak and fickle." In Eve "The whole female sex transgressed."[10] St. Augustine, glossing St. Paul's teaching, grapples with the condition of woman in relation to God: "Have women not the renewal of the mind in which is the image of God? Who would say this? But in the sex of their body they do not signify this. . . . The part . . . which they signify in the very fact of their being women, is that which may be called the concupiscential part."[11] Augustine's own unruly concupiscence is the base of his misogyny — half a lifetime spent in what Shakespeare would call "The expense of spirit in a waste of shame" (Sonnet CXXIX). He was converted from his carnal pursuits, but the object of those pursuits is made into the cause, the occasion of sin. As such, woman is unredeemable. His definitions of woman partake of his own sordid conduct and are direct projections of his own guilty style of life. Augustine goes on to explain how Paul's teaching does not contradict *Genesis'* statement that male and female are created in God's image. With gordian-knot casuistry he explains that because human nature is complete only in both sexes, of course, the writer of *Genesis* did not separate woman from the image of God. What St. Paul clarifies about *Genesis*, says Augustine, is a subtle point: "The woman together with her husband is the image of God; but when she is referred to separately in her quality of helpmate, which regards the woman herself alone, then she is not the image of God; but as regards the man alone, he is in the image of God as fully and completely as when the woman too is joined with him."[12] That such ratiocination could be taken seriously is a measure of the church's deep-rooted problem of injustice toward women. Considering the stature of Augustine and the reverence with which his teachings are unselectively promulgated to this day, one gets a clearer idea of the official opinion on women in the male-dominated church of seventeenth-century Rome.

The first systemization of canon law, the *Decretum* of 1140, declares:

> Women should be subject to their men. The natural order for mankind is that women should serve men, . . . for it is just that the lesser serve the greater.
>
> The image of God is in man and it is one. Women were drawn from man, who has God's jurisdiction as if he were God's vicar, because he has the image of the one God. Therefore woman is not made in God's image. Woman's authority is nil; let her in all things be subject to the rule of man. . . . And neither can she teach, nor be a witness, nor give guarantee, nor

sit in judgment. Adam was beguiled by Eve, not she by him. It is right that he whom woman led into wrong-doing should have her under his direction, so that he may not fail a second time through female levity.[13]

The last paragraph, probably inadvertently, is an admission of masculine weakness in being duped by such an inferior intellect, not made in God's image. The suppression of women within the church is justified by these theological dissertations: she is forbidden to teach; she is barred from the priesthood; she is denied entrance, except, significantly, at her wedding, into the sanctuary; may not touch the sacred vessels; is not permitted to sing in the choir. Thus, the custom of boy sopranos and castrati to perform the treble women do naturally.

In the great St. Thomas Aquinas, most esteemed of all theologians, nicknamed "The Angelic Doctor" with affection and awe, we see the recurrence of Aristotle's idea that woman is a flawed man: ". . . Woman is defective and misbegotten, for the active force in the male seed tends to the production of a perfect likeness in the masculine sex; while the production of woman comes from a defect in the active force or from some material indisposition, or even from some external influence. . . ."[14] Aquinas, like Paul and Chrysostom, admits the necessity of women as breeders of the human race, but Thomas goes so far as to verbalize *why* it was necessary that the first life produced from human generation was produced from wombless man: "When all things were first formed, it was more suitable for the woman to be made from the man," even though Aquinas concedes this is not the order of generation and did not so occur in any of the other animals. The reason why it is "more suitable" is blatantly stated in undisguised machismo: "First, in order to give the first man a certain dignity consisting in this, that as God is the principle of the whole universe, so the first man in likeness to God, was the principle of the whole human race. . . ."[15] The rationalization of the supremacy of man over woman is crowned by further reflections on the separate definition theme by now so entrenched in the Christian discourse. Aquinas adds his massive authority to the argument: "The image of God is found in man, and not in woman: for man is the beginning and end of woman; as God is the beginning and end of every creature."[16] In Christian theology the continually recurring analogy of man with God, inseparable from the separate definition argument, provides solid foundation and authority both for Guido's continued comparison of himself with God the Father,[17] and his arrogant devaluation of his wife. Count Franceschini is a perfect model and product of a theological tradition which has created a god in man's image. Browning's Pope sees this clearly and knows it must be changed:

> Correct the portrait by the living face,
> Man's God, by God's God in the mind of man.
> (x, 1872-3)

From Thomas Aquinas one may not hear the roaring misogyny of the earlier Tertullian, but his teaching on women is no different in essence. In *De Cultu Feminarum*, Tertullian is particularly strident in his outright denunciation of women as the root of all evil: "And do you not know that you are Eve? God's sentence hangs still over all your sex and His punishment weighs down upon you. You are the devil's gateway; you are she who first violated the forbidden tree and broke the law of God. It was you who coaxed your way around him whom the devil had not the force to attack. With what ease you shattered the image of God: man! Because of the death you merited the Son of God had to die."[18] Some of the implications here surely are not intended. The celebrated image of God, man, comes across poorly as one so easily shattered by such an inferior being, woman. On the other hand, Tertullian attributes to woman a power of evil exceeding Satan's, for his angelic power was incapable of attacking man — "had not the force to attack" — whereas she shattered him with ease. The message to woman is, nonetheless, plain: You deserve whatever suffering you get; it is all directly from God as just punishment. Many a rapist has reasoned thus. What we see so consistently in these time-honored teachers, on many of whom their religious establishment has conferred sainthood, is the voice and mentality of the extreme misogyny of the pornographer.

Clement of Alexandria, for example, reflects that "it brings shame even to reflect of what nature [woman] is. . . ."[19] Such reflection brings shame to whom? Reflecting on what her nature is in itself does not bring shame to a woman. Reflecting on her nature as seen and defined by a misogynistic male vision inevitably brings her shame, for it is the image of woman as inferior, objectified, without soul, without the divine image—in St. Paul's words, something "made for the man"; it is the pornographer's vision and definition of woman. It is intrinsically humiliating to her. Thus, a woman cannot read these texts consecrated by church tradition without humiliation. By highest religious authorities she is instructed to shame: she is the occasion of sin, the gate of hell, Eve, Pandora. The history of Christian theology and the history of pornography are manifestly bonded by a shared image of woman.[20] The bond is blatantly evident in the social ambience of Guido Franceschini and the church of seventeenth-century Rome so graphically delineated by Browning. For Pompilia it was a coil to destroy her, body and soul. Her husband was a perfect exemplar of a mentality destructive to her precisely in her nature as a woman and her function as a wife. A centuries-old brotherhood provided support for Guido both as secular nobleman and minor cleric.

Guido as Husband

What exactly was Guido's treatment of his wife? We have seen his attitude toward Pompilia, and indeed toward all women, in his first monologue in Book V. Pompilia had for twelve years led a very sheltered life with her adoptive parents, Violante and Pietro Comparini.

She was loved by this ageing couple, so long childless, somewhat in the untroublesome way grandparents love the children of their off-spring. Unpropitious as her real parentage was, this issue of a run-down prostitute and a nameless drifter was brought up in an environment of loving kindness by the Comparini. She was beautiful and, through adoption, had wealth coming to her as the only heir of a prosperous middle-class inheritor of a substantial fortune. The stupid, scheming Violante used the wealth as bait to secure nobility for her daughter through marriage. Because the greed of the Franceschini was akin to her own, Violante was blinded. She did not trouble her-self to discern the character of the husband to whom she was bridling her child. Count Guido Franceschini was indeed to be a groom who would treat Pompilia as a bridled horse.

The young wife, for all her inexperience, made strong judgments concerning whatever impinged on her sense of self. Indeed, Pompilia's sense of self is the key to her morality. Yet this young girl was no rebel. Brought up in an untroubled home, she was taught and ac-cepted the conventional attitudes toward marriage: that it was a girl's fulfillment and guarantor of protection and joy. She did not expect betrayal and abandonment by her parents nor brutalization by her husband. Looking back from her deathbed, she reflects:

> So with my husband, —just such a surprise,
> Such a mistake, in that relationship!
> Everyone says that husbands love their wives,
> Guard them and guide them, give them happiness;
> 'Tis duty, law, pleasure, religion: well,
> You see how much of this comes true in mine!
> (VII, 150-5)

All Guido's malevolence toward his wife took the form of sexual debasement, first in private, then with the attempt to bring her to public shame and humiliation, but in every case ultimate damnation was the goal. Guido's hatred wanted an eternal meal: he wished to corrupt Pompilia's soul through corruption of her body. Pompilia notes Guido's "dreadfully honest" statement:

>   'Since our souls
> Stand each from each, a whole world's width between,
> Give me the fleshly vesture I can reach
> And rend and leave just fit for hell to burn!'
> (VII, 781-4)

The internal riming and multiple alliteration of stops and fricatives perfectly capture Guido's tone and embody the intensity of his message which has burned itself into her memory. There is no attempt to seduce her into compliance with mere lust. His plan is rape. She sees the full implication of his words, understands he means to break her morally, kill her soul through pollution of her body:

> Why, in God's name, for Guido's soul's own sake
> Imperilled by polluting mine, — I say,
> I did resist; would I had overcome!
> (VII, 785-7)

In Pompilia's account of her sexual relations with Guido, one finds only a recording of forced intercourse which she will not name and finds it difficult to relate. As she lies dying from multiple stab wounds, she seems to ignore these, yet suffers anew to recount the progress of her brutal sexual initiation at the hands of Guido. Addressing the predominantly female audience around her deathbed, Pompilia begs her listeners to "Try to take the sense / Of what I signify," or "Women as you are, how can I find the words?" She wants them to understand the full significance of her words. Her narrative, as one would expect from a dying person in severe physical pain, moves back and forth on a continuum of time past, a speculation of time potential — what might have been — and at last an assumption into an eternal present. Her narration does not come in chronological order, and the audience must piece together a segmented account of her life with Guido. But she speaks from the moment of truth, her imminent death, and her narrative has the moral elevation, incisive clarity, and toughness of judgment associated with such a moment. Her account is no idle rambling, moreover, for she has been enjoined by her confessor, Fra Celestine, to resuscitate the past, recall in detail the prolonged abuse by her murderer in order that she truly might forgive him. For her own salvation she must face with experiential knowledge the evil done to her, and which she has suppressed from consciousness and memory, before she truly can wipe it out with forgiveness. Only in obedience to this directive does Pompilia recount the progress of the marriage, how her debasement began and developed. It seems she was ignored for the first few weeks of her residence in the House of Franceschini, while Guido and her parents wrangled over the fulfillment of the contract. During this time she unwittingly became the vicarious object of Guido's hatred for the Comparini. Too young and inexperienced to know there was such conflict, Pompilia never entered the dispute as a proper wife to take her husband's part. She had been kept in total ignorance that she had been a pawn in the marriage arrangement, yet looking back she judges both husband and parents with incisive moral vision:

> I was blind.
> That is the fruit of all such wormy ways,
> The indirect, the unapproved of God:
> You cannot find their author's end and aim.
> (VII, 668-71)

Frustrated in not getting the expected cash along with his bride, Guido decided to get full measure from the property at hand, and turned toward Pompilia with what Caponsacchi later describes as "some lust, letch of hate against his wife" (VI, 1796). Pompilia is far into her monologue when she recounts the precise instance of initiation into the rites of this marriage:

> Remember I was barely twelve years old—
> A child at marriage: I was let alone
> For weeks, I told you, lived my child-life still
> Even at Arezzo, when I woke and found
> First . . . but I need not think of that again—
> Over and ended! Try to take the sense
> Of what I signify, if it must be so.
> (VII, 734-40)

The ellipsis here is her own, and accompanies every explicit reference to sexual intercourse with Guido.

Browning's style frequently baffles. Its movement from the cryptic, to the diffuse, to the opaque, to the unsaid demands a great deal of the reader in crucial places. For Pompilia's psychological inability to name or describe Guido's treatment of her, Browning supplies the key in other parts of her dialogue and in words recounted in Caponsacchi's testimony in Book VI. The priest tells of a nightmare Pompilia had in the carriage after she, out of fear, refused to stop for much needed rest at Foligno. In her sleep she cried out to Guido:

> 'Never again with you!
> My soul is mine, my body is my soul's:
> You and I are divided evermore
> In soul and body: get you gone!'
> (VI, 1295-8)

She spoke with such violent intensity in her dismissal of the shade of Guido that Caponsacchi's response was a prayer of exorcism. Guido seemed thus dispelled from her dreams for she sank into peace by morning. Her language had a profound effect on Caponsacchi who, because of Pompilia's reserve, could only have guessed at Guido's explicitly sexual degradation of his wife implied in her "Never again with you!" The language of exorcism is the medium of Pompilia's address to her husband, dreaming or waking. Caponsacchi recounts how, when Guido confronted her at Castelnuovo with, "Behold the poisoner, the adulteress" (VI, 1521), Pompilia cried out:

> 'Away from between me and hell! . . .
> Hell for me, no embracing any more!
> I am God's, I love God, God—whose knees I clasp,
> Whose utterly most just award I take,
> But bear no more love-making devils: hence!'
> (VI, 1528-32)

To her, what the world calls love-making is hell, and its maker a devil. This speech echoes her nightmare cry in its estimate of her sexual life with Guido, and its exorcism of her husband as the agent of hell. Her calmer speech on her deathbed, cited above (VII, 734-40), partakes, nevertheless, of this language of dismissal: immediately following the ellipsis—"First . . ."—Pompilia represses the thought of what is not expressed—"but I need not think of that again"—and peremptorily dismisses it—"Over and ended!"—while begging her listeners to infer significance from her very reticence.

In his testimony Guido blames his wife as provoker of her husband's abuse. He claims she could have softened him by compliance, but his wife

> Would not begin the lie that ends with truth,
> Nor feign the love that brings true love about:
> Wherefore I judged, sentenced and punished her.
> (XI, 1428-30)

Pompilia, however, sees her conduct in a different light altogether:

> I am blamed that I forwent
> A way to make my husband's favor come.
> That is true: I was firm, withstood, refused . . .
> —Women as you are, how can I find the words?

> I felt there was just one thing Guido claimed
> I had no right to give nor he to take;
> We being in estrangement, soul from soul.
> (VII, 717-23)

Pompilia has a sexual creed inseparable from her total sense of personal morality, and surely not taught by her culture. To consummate with her body a love that did not exist would be a betrayal of truth and, consequently, a violation of self. She firmly believed in the justice and the moral necessity of her refusal to consummate her marriage. Her resolve was not sanctioned by the church, however, and in seeking help from the Archbishop of Arezzo after her sexual initiation, Pompilia is scolded into compliance. After "inquiring into the privacies of life," the Archbishop smiled and said she was blamable, "Nowise entitled to exemption there." Pompilia's compliance is based solely on the moral authority of the Archbishop who, in her own words, "stands for God." But she learns that her obedience to him is a betrayal of self, and Pompilia makes a startling statement of moral perception: "Then I obeyed. . . ."

> But I did wrong, and he gave wrong advice
> Though he were thrice Archbishop, — that I know!
> (VII, 731-2)

Her conviction comes from experiential knowledge. What she experiences from Guido she explains in a powerfully telling analogy. She sees her life with Guido as a shorter version of, but essentially the same as her mother's life of prostitution. Pompilia claims affinity and understanding in mutual degradation:

> My own real mother, whom I never knew,
> Who did wrong . . .
> Through being all her life, not my four years,
> At mercy of the hateful, — every beast

O' the field was wont to break that fountain-fence,
Trample the silver into mud so murk
Heaven could not find itself reflected there.
(VII, 864-70)

Trial proceedings had, of course, brought publicity to Pompilia's dis-
honorable parentage, and public opinion judged her accordingly. Just
as people compare her with her mother, so does she herself, but with
an ironic perspective:

Well since she had to bear this brand — let me!
The rather do I understand her now, —
From my experience of what hate calls love.
(VII, 874-6)

In marriage Pompilia has experienced the degradation of a prostitute.

A terrible intimation of what was in store for the bride can be seen
in Abate Paolo Franceschini's wedding homily, a distracted, cynical,
glib, confused pastiche of Christ's parables and miracles. The miracle
of the marriage feast at Cana is pragmatically debased into an analogy
concerning woman's worth. In herself she is water; as a wife she is
wine — turned into a delectable substance because of union with a husband from whence alone she receives value and honor, and to whom
that value is due. Her value, just as it does not come from herself, but,
from her husband, is not for herself, but, like food, exists for the consumption of her husband. Paolo's crude analogy is not isolated. It
recurs over and over in other actors of the drama, most notably in the
Archbishop's second bit of counsel to the erring wife.

After her initial disillusion in the Archbishop, Pompilia is once
more driven to his feet by fear of new cruelties from her husband.
Immediately following her account of her sexual initiation, Pompilia
goes on to recount Guido's announcement of a second phase in their
relations. Again, the treatment she expects is implied, not stated
directly:

> After the first, my husband, for hate's sake,
> Said one eve, when the simpler cruelty
> Seemed somewhat dull at edge and fit to bear,
> 'We have been man and wife six months almost:
> How long is this your comedy to last?
> Go this night to my chamber not to your own!
> (VII, 741-6)

These words of Guido drive her at once to the Archbishop for help, imploring him to allow her to leave her husband and enter a convent to live a life consecrated to chastity. Again her words imply the one thing she cannot bear from Guido — sexual intercourse: "what my estranged soul / Refused to bear, though patient of the rest" (VII, 750-1). She feels her soul imperilled by further sexual degradation. Her experience, rather than her imagination, is the only source of her interpretation of Guido's command. This interview with the Archbishop is recounted in cinematic detail, so deeply did his words and gestures instill desperation and helplessness into his young supplicant. The prelate's response to her frantic plea is an attempt at casuistic instruction concerning the respective values of virginity and motherhood, which, failing to move, he turns to a brutal rebuff: "'Twas in your covenant!'" In other words, Guido's treatment of her, which he knows in detail, having inquired "into privacies of life," no matter how degrading, is in the marriage contract as recognized and blessed by the church. Thinking of what she had been through already and the new fear that drove her to the feet of the Archbishop, Pompilia sees the hopelessness of having recourse to such a morally opaque source:

> My heart died out at the Archbishop's smile;
> — It seemed so stale and worn a way o' the world,
> As though 't were nature frowning. . . .
> (VII, 787-90)

As the interview builds in tension, he takes the Count's part unequivocally. Privy to all the details of their marital relations — "More than I dared make my own mother know" — the Archbishop puts the authority of his office behind his support for Guido, becoming savage in his impatience toward Pompilia:

> Last he said, savagely for a good man,
>   ... 'God's Bread!
> The poor Count has to manage a mere child
> Whose parents leave untaught the simplest things
> Their duty was and privilege to teach, —
> Goodwives' instruction, gossips' lore: they laugh
> And leave the Count the task — or leave it me!'
> (VII, 798-803)

His refusal to assess Guido's treatment of his wife in its true light forces Pompilia to reveal another "frightful thing" — the attempts of Girolamo, her priest brother-in-law, to seduce her with Guido's total acquiescence: "Is it your counsel I bear this beside?" The barb in Pompilia's question hits home and the prelate snaps at her, "More scandal, and against a priest this time!" By way of conciliation the prelate goes on to instruct Pompilia as an erring child on her proper marital role. He tells a gruesome parable about a "ripe round long black toothsome fruit," a flower-fig commanded by the gardener, "Archbishop of the orchard" or the "Creator's self," to yield herself up as food for a bird:

> 'Ripe fig, burst skin, regale the fig-pecker —
> The bird whereof thou art a perquisite!'
> (VII, 831-2)

The fig, refusing to yield to "the natural lord," was beset by "three hundred thousand bees and wasps" who "feasted on her to the shuck: ... the moral, — fools elude their proper lot. ... Therefore go home, embrace your husband quick!" (VII, 839-44). The crudeness of the parable and the diction of its narration betray an attitude shared by Guido and the Archbishop: a wife is for the consumption of the husband, her sexuality for him to use as he wills. Woman's "proper lot" is to pleasure man.

Pompilia's narration of this interview shows an increasingly critical distancing of herself from this man to whom she had had recourse for spiritual direction. Her reproduction of his tone, his cynicism, his worldliness and complete complicity in the sexual debasement of her marriage manifests a definite moral judgment of him. At the end of the interview she is alone, but on a moral eminence—responsible for herself alone and to God whose values she divorces from the Archbishop, whom her entire culture and upbringing had taught her to accept as God's representative:

> So home I did go; so, the worst befell:
> So I had proof the Archbishop was just man,
> And hardly that, and certainly no more.
> (VII, 847-9)

Experience leads Pompilia to a pinnacle of self-direction and moral responsibility, even in this most diminished state when "my last stay and comfort in myself / Was forced from me" (VII, 853-4). The maturity manifested here is impressive indeed. What Pompilia sees and evaluates according to her own insight is the utter worthlessness and cant of institutionalized religion and marriage. The institutions are products of man, not God, in spite of their constant use of God as inventor and upholder of these institutions. She sees with moral clarity the undifferentiation of the church and the state, for after recounting her judgment of the Archbishop she recalls her subsequent visit, in desperation, to the Governor. He had railed at her earlier for selling a jewel or two—gifts from her parents—to feed the now destitute Comparini couple. The jewels, said the Governor, belonged to her husband as did all her possessions, including herself. Even so, she had recourse to him as a last authority:

Yet being in extremity, I fled
To the Governor, as I say, — scarce opened lip
When — the cold cruel snicker close behind —
Guido was on my trace, already there,
Exchanging nod and wink for shrug and smile.
(VII, 1275-9)

Yet again the conspiracy of virilism closes in on her, and Guido, it seems clear, punishes her by rape. Pompilia's statement is punctuated by the usual hallmark of ellipsis followed by dismissal from memory:

And I — pushed back to him and, for my pains,
Paid with . . . but why remember what is past?
(VII, 1280-1)

Pompilia's summation of the conduct of both the Archbishop and the Governor — the supreme spiritual and civil authorities of the city — bears out the words of the poet in Book I, where he saw Arezzo as "the man's town / The woman's trap and cage and torture-place" (I, 501-2). She completely understands the impenetrable fortress of patriarchy, and wisely comments on the hopelessness of putting any trust in its institutions and representatives:

Prayers move God; threats, and nothing else, move men!
I must have prayed a man as he were God
When I implored the Governor to right
My parents' wrongs: the answer was a smile.
The Archbishop, — did I clasp his feet enough,
Hide my face hotly on them, while I told
More than I dared make my own mother know?
The profit was — compassion and a jest.
(VII, 1624-31)

Pompilia Comparini feels particularly betrayed by the Archbishop because he drew from her the details of her sexual degradation. Her obedience to his probing is due entirely and solely to the spiritual authority vested in his office. To recount one's rape, in or out of marriage, is itself degrading, reviving the victimization through shame. Pompilia, as we have seen, maintains consistent reticence in this regard. She is not explicit with the auditors on her deathbed. She does not give an account of it to Caponsacchi when she tries to explain the extremity of her position in the House of Franceschini. She tells him that she had confided to her confessor, the monk Romano, "What I never will tell you" (VI, 842). As with the Archbishop, her confiding to her confessor was for the sole purpose of securing deliverance. The costliness of her revelation to the Archbishop is dramatically implied by her diction: "the *profit* was—compassion and a jest." Nor does she gain any profit from her outlay of emotional and spiritual expense to Fra Romano who, though he sympathizes with her and considers her conjugal treatment as "outrageous," sees it as no more than the common lot of woman (VI, 838-41). He is disturbed only by the sexual solicitations from the priest Girolamo. Romano's failure to see her condition is rooted in the same place as his failure to help his supplicant: acceptance of the bond between men who see women as expendable. By accepting the way things are, he is assenting to them. The friar thus participates in and supports the very suppression of women he compassionates in Pompilia. His failure to help her is based in this acceptance. He is an unqualified participant in the complicity of oppressive virilism. The failure of this truly pious and unworldly source of help drives Pompilia deeper into despair, for she sees the whole world turned to support her ultimate moral destruction.

When one looks at Guido's words about marriage or about human sexuality in general, one sees the evil of institutional or societal complicity in its support of him. In the condemned murderer's final testament he brags to the attending clergy about his attitude toward his wife: "Here's my slave, / Whose body and soul depend upon my nod" (XI, 1418-9). He uses *Genesis* to justify his assessment of a wife's role: "Thy desire / Shall be to the husband, o'er thee shall he rule!" (XI, 1304-5). With the mounting confidence of cynicism he gives the time-honored pornographic image of wife as horse—she should obey, not for love, but from powerlessness:

> . . . Where's the bond obliges horse to man
> Like that which binds fast wife to husband? God
> Laid down the law: gave man the brawny arm
> And ball of fist—woman the beardless cheek
> And proper place to suffer in the side:
> Since it is he can strike, let her obey!
> Can she feel no love? Let her show the more,
> Sham the worse, damn herself praiseworthily!
> (XI, 1400-7)

Interestingly enough, the Count agrees with his wife in this matter. He definitely judges as self-damning a wife's sexual cooperation where she feels no love. Guido, who understands and flaunts his purpose in degrading his wife, is more honest than the official clergy, who, knowing intimately the cause of Pompilia's desperation, dismiss it as the proper lot of women and therefore incontestable.

Before leaving the subject of Guido as a spouse, it would be enlightening to look into his imaginative ramblings. His sexual fantasies are expressed in Book XI where he defines his idea of a real woman in contrast to Pompilia. The stream of consciousness in his last monologue reveals an amazing landscape of Guido's mind and moral sensibility. He launches his speech with a long rumination about the guillotine, studded with sardonic gallows humor, but woven through with a horrifying story in praise of class injustice superimposed on sexual exploitation. He narrates how the sister of a certain buffalo keeper, Felice, was abducted by the Duke. Felice in outrage struck at the Duke in order to defend his sister's honor:

> Because he kidnapped, carried away and kept
> Felice's sister that would sit and sing. . . .
> The good girl with the velvet in her voice.
> (XI, 200-1, 204)

For his pains, Felice was beheaded. And Guido, bent on his own defense for treating a woman as a possession, reveals more levels of his sordid attitude toward his wife. In using the Felice story, however, Guido seems to have short-circuited his logic because of the apparent lack of parallelism. He is, after all, complaining of the alleged abduction of his own wife by the priest Caponsacchi. But he is illustrating not only the expendability of women but also the privilege of nobility. The two concepts are inseparable. Felice loses his sister; the kidnapper is a nobleman; therefore the abductor is justified. The privilege of nobility is apparent, assumed. Women are fair game. But the point Guido seems to be making is that society concurred, approved of the Duke's right to abduct Felice's sister and execute the objecting brother, her only defense. Guido, as nobleman, feels betrayed in his own case. Like the Duke, he has done no more than execute those troublesome to him, yet he is condemned. "Why do things change? Wherefore is Rome un-Romed?" (XI, 265). He reinforces his illustration by the sequel, telling how, after Felice's execution,

> The Duke, that night, threw wide his palace-doors,
> Received the compliments o' the gentry,
> For justice done him.
> (XI, 267-9)

In return for their adulation, the Duke smirkingly rewards them with a "pretty thing" (XI, 270), passing around a pornographic painting — "Florid old rogue Albano's masterpiece" — posed for by Felice's sister (XI, 272). That Felice's sister — significantly nameless — is sexually corrupted as well as sexually exploited is a comfort and a triumph to the group. The company show their appreciation by laughter, "and took their leave safelier home," relieved of the threat to their way of life.

Pope Alexander VII, Guido notes nostalgically, would have enjoyed such a story: "Ah, but times change, there's quite another Pope,

/ I do the Duke's deed, take Felice's place, . . ." and for his attention to duty, receives a sentence for murder. Browning's use of this story and his recreation of the sordid ambience of the shared dirty joke places Guido among his moral peers in a way that no other device could. The sexual cynicism of a bonded male in a patriarchal culture and the assured privilege of a nobleman in a class society are the ballasts of Guido's argument. The values upon which his justification depends — values bolstered by society and religion — are those of power. A man's honor is rooted in the subjugation of the powerless. Thus he can claim early on in his final testimony that

> . . . All honest Rome approved my part;
> Whoever owned wife, sister, daughter, — nay
> Mistress, — had any shadow of any right
> That looks like right, and, all the more resolved,
> Hold it with tooth and nail, — these manly men
> Approved! I being for Rome, Rome was for me!
> (XI, 39-40)

His final chiasmus here reinforces an irony and a truth: he, a Tuscan, despises Rome, but in this point about the subjugation of women both societies concur.

Particularly revealing is another of Guido's rambling illustrations to assess the value of women. Having identified the "manly men" who approve of his violence, he excoriates the bad taste of "you other kind of men" (XI, 2109) who side with Pompilia as victim. His contempt for the poor taste of men who can value such a woman is telling. Assessing Pompilia as a saint, these men seem to taunt Guido as one who does not know how to value a painting: "Why, 't is a Raphael that you kicked to rags!" (XI, 2115). His retort adheres to the painting metaphor appropriately maintaining the universal attitude of possession as well as revealing his own taste in women:

> Perhaps so: some prefer the pure design:
> Give me my gorge of color, glut of gold
> In a glory round the Virgin made for me!
> Titian's the man, not Monk Angelico. . . .
> (XI, 2116-9)

One hears the contempt spat out in the heavily alliterated plosives of the first line. Then follows the food metaphor further sensualized by the heavy alliteration of gutturals describing the kind of saint made for his possession. The most cursory look at the respective paintings of Titian and Fra Angelico illustrates how consistent with Guido's character is his artistic predilection. Titian supplied his wealthy clients, such as the Duke Guidobaldo II of Urbino and King Philip II of Spain, with ample pornography including lush romanticization and glorification of rape.[21] These depictions of reclining naked women are, of course, baptized with classical and historical titles, but they manifest a way of seeing women, shared by the artist and his client and his admirers. It is the way certain men see women; it is not a vision shared by women. Guido is surely part of an age-old brotherhood. As one writer explains: "The female nude, painted by men, becomes the icon for a culture which is defined as exclusively male."[22] Charlotte Bronte deals with this bond in her last novel, *Villette*, when Lucy Snowe amusingly reflects upon men's obvious relish in a voluptuous painting of Cleopatra which her male companions think it indecent of her, as a woman, to look upon.[23] When Edouard Manet exposed this bond with his "Olympia" in 1863, the established art critics were not amused.[24] As always, Guido is no such pretender. His allusion to Titian leads him into a long disquisition on his assessment of women.

What Guido describes—"Give them me! / O those Olimpias bold, the Biancas brave" (XI, 1282)—is the quintessential man's woman. He sees her very specifically, as one who reveals that her only function is to give pleasure to men, particularly the pleasure of lust.

Guido's ideal is the woman who cries to him, "Why, what but thine am I" (XI, 2184), and goes on to proclaim,

> 'Be thou to me law, right, wrong, heaven and hell!
> Let us blend souls, be thou in me to bid
> Two bodies work one pleasure!'
> (XI, 2185-7)

As the valiant helpmate, she offers at his bidding to murder his enemies, be they "Called king, father, mother, stranger, friend" (XI, 2189). He has her fantasize how to use her sexuality to seduce his enemy, so that he can murder him more conveniently. She claims to be at once his trained falcon and his reward:

> 'What is a man to me
> Who am thy call-bird? Twist his neck — my dupe's —
> Then take the breast shall turn a breast indeed!'
> (XI, 2201-3)

Guido, creating this woman, pronounces with self-righteous conviction, "Such women are there" (XI, 2204), and indeed it is obvious that they are familiar figures in the blue pages of the speaker's mind. He goes on to ask whom these women marry, and it is significant that Guido, to procure such a prize, must turn, not to real life — the world of real woman, but to hell. He fairly salivates as he is drawn deeper and deeper into his fantasy, moving from the vision of the seductress Circe as "perfection" to the embodiment of woman-as-sin in Lucretia Borgia, who will teach him "Sin unimagined, unimaginable" (XI, 2216). In a virtual ecstasy of sin he cries out to his created vision,

> I am come to claim my bride — thy Borgia's self
> Not half the burning bridegroom I shall be!
> (XI, 2217-8)

Guido truly is united in fantasy to his vision of woman-as-sin. He chooses for his ideal bride the monstrously evil, steeped-in-sin image of woman embodied in the Lucretia Borgia mythology. His particular form of pleasure will be to master her, outdo her evil with his own. As his fantasizing breaks out into this absorbing vocative, the attending cardinal breaks in with his crucifix in a gesture of exorcism. The act is an assessment and a judgment of Guido's sexual morality. Here Guido's open articulation of the pornographic vision cannot be shared for it is not disguised. Pompilia always gave her husband credit for his honesty in his sexual abuse of her—"Hate was thus the truth of him" (VII, 1727). He is no less forthright here in his fantasizing of the feminine ideal. Inappropriate as it might seem for Guido to be indulging in his lurid fantasy on the brink of death to two clerical attendants, the misogynistic attitude manifested therein is entirely in keeping with the values dominating his culture and his religion. He is indeed and in truth Count Guido Franceschini, nobleman of Arezzo, and a cleric ordained in minor orders in the Roman church.[25]

That Guido was condemned to death for his murders, that his plea of *honoris causa* was dismissed, that his wife was vindicated from the charge of adultery are an extraordinary set of circumstances. In spite of the eight months of testimony and the arguments of a cumulated culture behind him, Guido was defeated by the truth and goodness of his victim. In Pompilia Guido says he hates ". . . this unmanly appetite for truth, / This careless courage as to consequences" (XI, 171-2). But the court weighs the respective values of this husband and this wife differently:

> We pronounce
> Count Guido devilish and damnable:
> His wife Pompilia in thought, word and deed
> Was perfect, pure, he murdered her for that.
> (I, 246-9)

Yet even after the sentence was pronounced, during the time of appeal, the general opinion was that Guido would be set free. He was aligned with the church through minor orders; he had appealed to the highest church authority for pardon; he would be dealt with as a loyal son of the church whose values he exemplified. " 'T was plain that Guido would go scatheless yet" (I, 294). In appeal Guido claimed his clericality, and

> 'Once the word "clericality" let fall,
> Procedure stopped and freer breath was drawn
> By all considerate and responsible Rome.'
> Quality took the decent part, of course;
> Held by the husband, who was noble too.
> (I, 273-7)

"Considerate" and "responsible" Rome, as we have seen, was trained since the beginning of Western Civilization to give men the mastery over women. In his long passage summarizing the arguments of Civilization in Guido's defense, the Pope delivers Civilization's principal argument to him:

> 'Take
> Count Guido's life, and sap society,
> Whereof the main prop was, is, and shall prove
> —Supremacy of husband over wife!'
> (X, 2031-4)

The Pope is not deaf to nor undiscerning of the language of doxology, used so pervasively and naturally by Guido as a spokesman of his culture, and used here in his defense by Civilization. He notes, with irony, how the culture does indeed speak. Its institutions are given divine reverence, its own image divine tribute. Just as Guido exemplifies the whole tradition of religiously justified misogyny, the supremely authoritative voice of *The Ring and the Book*, Browning's Pope Innocent,[26] is exemplar and spokesman for a completely contrary ideal, "the new order of things" (X, 1910). So too Pompilia, in rejecting

Guido's treatment of her, in rejecting the advice of the Governor and
Archbishop to be "some bone for him to mumble," (X, 1462) rejects
the long tradition of teaching about the woman's God-ordained role
to pleasure men. She sees her husband's plotting to corrupt her as an
attempt to make her unselve herself. It is her strong sense of self-
possession that Guido cannot penetrate and to which he gives, in the
end, grudging tribute:

> This self-possession to the uttermost,
> How does it differ in aught, save degree,
> From the terrible patience of God?
> (XI, 1376-8)

The character Browning has created in Guido's wife, Pompilia Comparini, grows through her trials from a docile child to a self-possessed,
determined woman "strong as stone," in Guido's words (XI, 1312). In
drawing such a detailed picture of the culture she rejects, the poet
gives us a measure of Pompilia's uniqueness and self-direction. Her
moral decisions are entirely contrary to every source of authority in
her life: husband, Governor, and Archbishop. That the Pope was
"Heartsick at having all his world to blame" (X, 1007) for her victimization was something she did not live to know and something
beyond her need to know, though it would have given her immeasurable consolation.

3 THE FIRST
EXPERIMENTALISTS

Correct the portrait by the living face,
Man's God, by God's God in the mind of man.
(X, 1872-3)

Surely some one Pompilia in the world
Will say, 'I know the right place by foot's feel,
I took it and tread from there; wherefore
    change?'
(X, 1884-6)

Can he teach others how to quit themselves,
Prove why this step was right, while that were
    wrong?
How should he? 'Ask your hearts as I asked
    mine. . . .'
(X, 1921-3)

So, never I miss footing in this maze,
No, — I have light nor fear the dark at all.
(X, 1658-9)

NOT ONLY DO three characters—Pompilia, Caponsacchi, and Pope Innocent XII—stand apart from the mainstream of seventeenth-century Rome; they decidedly stand counter. By their decisions, their actions, their frames of mind, they make definitive judgments on the universal assent to woman's devaluation, exemplified so dramatically in the institutions of marriage and the church. So radical are their positions of denial, even denunciation, of the *status quo*, that these three seem to signal a new order of things. The old order is well-exemplified, articulated, and summed up by the two lawyers whose monologues are beautifully juxtaposed to the Pope's; and, before examining the three deviants from this order, it would be beneficial to glimpse briefly its official legal spokesmen.

Amid all the gossip, opinions, hearsay, defenses, exonerations, and condemnations comprising the monologues of *The Ring and the Book*, only three voices represent contemporary legal judgments of the Franceschini crime and its principals: those of Archangelis (Book VIII), Bottinius (Book IX), and the Pope (Book X). Pompilia Comparini and Giuseppe Caponsacchi had taken a radical stand outside accepted law, civil and ecclesiastical, and the law at the first trial had condemned them with dispatch. When their illegal conduct once more comes under scrutiny because of Guido's murder trial, they are again seen as guilty by both trial lawyers, even the Fisc, who as Guido's prosecutor, must somehow place Pompilia's behavior in a favorable light. The Pope, on the other hand, instantly and unequivocally perceives the pair as innocent throughout. It is obvious that the lawyers and the Pope speak from two different worlds: they from the world of *honoris causa*; he from the world of moral responsibility into which Pompilia and Caponsacchi have entered, and into which he had passed long ago. That the Pope speaks immediately after the two advocates is dramatically and artistically brilliant. The lawyer's speeches are gems of legalese setting up the crowning jewel of the poem, the Pope's ultimate moral judgment of Guido and all the willing and unwilling participants in his drama. Both lawyers' monologues provide a riotous brand of mirth. Browning has a mind for mirth, and, like all good comedians, sees the exposure of human folly as a powerful prospectus on morality. The poet knows exactly what he is doing with this pair of publicly elevated professionals. In his engaging correspondence with Julia Wedgwood over the composition of *The Ring and the Book*, Browning explains: "The buffoon lawyers (not a bit, intellectually or morally, beneath lawyers I have known) serve an artistic purpose and let you breathe a little before the last vial is poured out."[1] Both lawyers are absurd as they prepare their briefs for the forthcoming trial, and they both speak from and exemplify the cultural absurdity delineated in the preceding chapter. Comics though they be, they are, nevertheless, products and nurturers of the world of Guido Franceschini, and Browning handles this affinity with a choice selection of detail.

In Archangelis' defense, resting on *honoris causa*, the lawyer waxes pompously on its sacrosanct character: ". . . Honour is a gift of God to man / Precious beyond compare" (VIII, 458-9), and quotes all the authorities, and more, cited in Chapter Two. Browning has him neatly show the complicity of antiquity and Christendom in the subjection of women while stating the main point of his defense of Guido:

> . . . then sustain the point—
> All that was long ago declared as law
> By the early Revelation, stands confirmed

> By Apostle and Evangelist and Saint, —
> To-wit — that Honour is the supreme good.
> (VIII, 579-83)

Next, by having Bottinius select for himself the metaphor of lawyer-as-artist, the poet deftly makes him reveal the complete spiritual kinship between the Fisc and Guido, prosecutor and criminal. The lawyer's predilection for canvases depicting in lush style such scenes as the trial of Phryne, the rape of Lucrecia, the stripping and chaining of Hesione for oblation, speaks for itself. With lurid relish he, of course, pictures Pompilia in these various guises. To him the dying woman is only a voluptuous and "splendidly mendacious" (IX, 836), "Thalassian-pure" Venus (891) — an art object to be possessed and ogled — a woman made for man.

Philip Drew considers "that the most powerful impression which Books VIII and IX make on the reader who knows nothing of Book X derives from their treatment of Pompilia."[2] Their treatment of her is one of total cynicism in shocking contrast to the values articulated and exemplified in the deathbed speech of Pompilia immediately preceding the lawyers' monologues. The lawyers illustrate a truth Pompilia sadly has learned from her experience with other human counsel. As Jerome L. Wyant has noted: "Implicit in both monologues is the idea that it is impossible to be corrupt in one area of activity without being depraved in others."[3] It is significant that Browning has the Pope speak immediately after these pompously comic buffoons and immediately before "the last vial is poured out" in Guido's final monologue. The Pope's soliloquy is the pinnacle separating two worlds: that of *honoris causa* and that of radical innocence. The world from and for which both lawyers speak is the world of Guido Franceschini — the world Pompilia will have no part in, the world Caponsacchi rescues her from and turns his own back upon, the world whose injustice burdens the heart of Browning's "great good old Pope" (I, 326).

In the sordid world of this novel, Pompilia, Caponsacchi, and the Pope are indeed "the first experimentalist[s] / In the new order of things" (X, 1909-10). They are good in a world of evil. What signals them so are their choices. Each of the three possesses a radical inno-cence— the innocence of the adult who chooses to turn from evil, the innocence attained by moral choices linked into a habit of goodness. When we first meet the Pope in Book X, he is habituated to a life of goodness. He possesses, or is possessed by, what the mystics would call "the habit of perfection." It is not so with either Caponsacchi or Pompilia. The priest moves from a state of restless acceptance of medi-ocrity to a heroic pursuit of truth and wholeness. The passage from one state to the other opens to Caponsacchi because of his agonized decision to rescue Pompilia. In Pompilia we see yet another kind of passage to the state of radical innocence. She moves from the ignorant innocence of the child when she refuses to accept her marital debase-ment. She moves from the hapless victim into a state of responsible adulthood when she decides to leave her husband. To stay with him was to choose damnation, disintegration of self. Her salvation comes with her costly choice. We do not know what constituted the passage for Antonio Pignatelli of Naples, now Pope Innocent XII, for we see him as an old man long habituated to truth. But in Caponsacchi and Pompilia we see quite different characters responding to their respec-tive moments of truth. Each of them, significantly, must make the radical choice alone with no help from normal societal sup-ports— parents, colleagues, civil and ecclesiastical authority. Indeed, the only counsel possible from such sources, as well demonstrated in both Pompilia's and Caponsacchi's cases, would be to prostitute one's truth to the inimical values of the world. Reliance on one's own limited faculties of judgment in adherence to absolute norms is, for them, the way to salvation, "Life's business being just the terrible choice" (X, 1237).

From Caponsacchi's first utterance (Book VI) and throughout the whole monologue, his sense of priesthood is manifest. When he begins the account of his life to the ecclesiastical court, his first words of self-definition are, "Yes, I am one of your body and a priest" (VI, 221). Ironically, Caponsacchi's sense of the priestly call is instilled, not at ordination when his superiors tried to vitiate it to nonentity, but at his first sight of Pompilia. Encounter with Pompilia—"the lady, young, tall, beautiful, strange and sad" (VI, 399)—does not send him on the romantic gambol everyone would cynically assume. He is powerfully and mysteriously affected by the sight of Guido Franceschini's sad wife in the theater with her menacing husband "lurking there i' the black o' the box" (VI, 414). Looking up at her he is transfixed, seeing her as a Raphael madonna, elevated above the carnival crowd, yet strangely in need. When he sees her next, in response to her summons, she is standing, a lamp in hand, framed in a black window of Guido's sinister house:

> Pompilia; the same great, grave, griefful air
> As stands i' the dusk, on altar that I know,
> Left alone with one moonbeam in her cells
> Our Lady of all the Sorrows.
> (VI, 704-7)

He almost kneels, so strong is his reflex of reverence. This is no residue of courtly love. What draws him is an overwhelming sense of her mysterious sorrow, her need for a strong friend. It seems that Caponsacchi's priesthood takes shape, becomes defined in a juxtaposition of his gifts, his strengths with her goodness, her helplessness:

> I had a whole store of strengths
> Eating into my heart, which craved employ,
> And she, perhaps, need of a finger's help, —
> And yet there was no way in the wide world
> To stretch out mine and so relieve myself.
> (VI, 495-9)

Never before had the priest been aware of his call to ministry, his need to serve the powerless. Pompilia's need defines his own vocation to service. Until the impact of that chance wordless encounter in the theater, Caponsacchi's sense of priesthood was desultory and hardly edifying. Yet originally his concept of vocation had been full of idealism. Primed since childhood for the priesthood, Caponsacchi, when the time came to read his vows, understood this, not as a meaningless act, but a grave commitment to "another life," a life of renunciation of the world (VI, 260-7). So strong was his sense of its magnitude that Caponsacchi, in his honesty and self-knowledge, demurred from such a step:

> I stopped short awe-struck. 'How shall holiest flesh
> Engage to keep such vow inviolate,
> How much less mine, — I know myself too weak,
> Unworthy! Choose a worthier stronger man!'
> (VI, 267-71)

The bishop, with affectionate cajolery allays the young man's fears, telling him that heroic renunciation was for a previous age, a time of martyrs and confessors who erected the buttress-work of the church. That having been done by heroic forebears, their present endeavor is simple maintenance and adornment:

> 'Renounce the world? Nay, keep it and give it us!
> Let us have you, and boast of what you bring;
> We want the pick of the earth to practise with. . . .'
> (VI, 309-11)

Giuseppe Caponsacchi is to grace the established church with his good looks, his noble family connections, his ability to charm and entertain. The bishop wants to brag about him as a good catch, to "tell the lady, 'And he's ours!' " (VI, 335). His scruples swept away by episcopal *fiat*, Caponsacchi went through his ordination to the priesthood.

And, though his standards were not the attainment of heroic sanctity and self-denial, he kept his vow:

> So I became a priest: those terms changed all,
> I was good enough for that, nor cheated so;
> I could live thus and still hold head erect.
> Now you see why I may have been before
> A fribble and coxcomb, yet a priest, break word
> Nowise, to make you disbelieve me now.
> I need that you should know my truth. . . .
> (VI, 336-42)

So Caponsacchi lived "according to prescription" (VI, 343), punctual to the appointed times of prayer and diligent to the post of fashion. Such a life in such a church insured advancement; Arezzo was a stepping stone to Rome and ecclesiastical promotion. As a child, was he not a "bishop in the egg" (VI, 258)? More so now, the new priest was being groomed for a position of power, his best assets for preferment being, according to his superiors,

> A polished presence, a genteel manner, wit
> At will, and tact at every pore of you!
> (VI, 371-2)

For three or four years the handsome canon was caught up in a life of spiritual sterility, in an endless round of paying court to gain and maintain a position in an institution that served only the rich and these only to its own ends. It is notable that the court he is addressing in Guido's trial is made up of just such men — men who have positions of power, getting them and holding them by the same methods in which Caponsacchi had been trained. Facing this court now he has only one purpose: to exonerate the dying Pompilia from the charge of adultery. When he says the impassioned words, "I need that you should know my truth," he is, for her sake, declaring the fact of his fidelity to his priestly vow, notwithstanding the former frivolity and shallowness of his daily life.

The sad image of Pompilia broke into that priestly charade, and Caponsacchi's life was transformed. His complacency disturbed, he starts to examine his own life and finds it wanting. Turning to prayer and meditation, he resolves to go to Rome, not to seek preferment, but to look into his own heart, to seek spiritual direction in a city presided over by "a strange Pope, . . . a priest who thinks" (VI, 478).

Just as Pompilia is the catalyst for Caponsacchi's change of orientation, so it is the knowledge of his plan to go to Rome that gives Pompilia her one concrete plan of escape. Caponsacchi's priestly life and Pompilia's married life have run parallel in time and place. While the virtually imprisoned Pompilia was imperiled in the house of the Franceschini, Caponsacchi was composing madrigals for the amusement of rich women. Both lives changed dramatically and irrevocably upon contact: Caponsacchi finds an outlet for priestly service; Pompilia finds a way to save herself, body and soul, and the life of her unborn child. It is significant that the priest's change of heart turns him toward Rome, not to seek promotion as planned, but to pursue a life of devotion and service—a priestly life. It is contact with Pompilia that turns him away from Arezzo to Rome; it is news of his planned exodus that turns Pompilia toward Caponsacchi as rescuer, providing him his first opportunity for useful service:

> You serve God specially, as priests are bound,
> And care about me, stranger as I am,
> So far as wish me good, — that miracle
> I take to intimate He wills you serve
> By saving me, — what else can He direct?
> Here is the service. . . .
> You go to Rome, they tell me: take me there
> Put me back with my people.
> (VII, 1429-34, 41-2)

He who intended Rome as a new source of priestly direction is given that direction before even setting out, not from the Pope, but from someone insignificant in the eyes of the church. Caponsacchi's quest becomes his end. It is precisely his priesthood that is the fulcrum and ballast of their flight to Rome. For the priest, rescue of this woman is a mandate from on high. It is, moreover, a right act, an act right for him, eminently fulfilling to his identity and calling:

> Pompilia spoke, and I at once received,
> Accepted my own fact, my miracle
> Self-authorised and self-explained, — she chose
> To summon me and signify her choice.
> (VI, 918-21)

Her choice is to throw off the yoke of victimization and despair and save herself and her unborn child through Caponsacchi's help. Pompilia's first adult joy comes with this decision:

> My heart sang, 'I too am to go away,
> I too have something I must care about,
> Carry away with me to Rome, to Rome!'
> (VII, 1237-9)

His choice is to throw off the yoke of the dandy and act the priest he is by serving her. Both see the priestly service as a miracle of unselfish love—to serve God in serving the stranger. It is Pompilia who perceives the miraculous nature of such service; Caponsacchi, the priest, receives his miracle from her summons. In both cases they discard and transcend a role imposed by their respective institutions —marriage and the church. Pompilia will not be a man's woman; Caponsacchi will no longer be a puppet priest. The only approval they will receive for their moral choices is from a man who holds to none of the values of society, that "strange Pope, . . . a priest who thinks" (VI, 478). In both cases their respective choices proceed from and lead to a heightened sense of self and of a transcendent God not made in man's image. By her choice to escape, Pompilia affirms "I have my purpose and my motive too / . . . How right to be alive!" (VII, 1245, 47). Pompilia's purpose is most surely not the one defined for her in the institution of marriage. By his choice to rescue her Caponsacchi accepts his own fact, "my miracle / Self-authorised and self-explained." His mission is far from the one defined for him in the institutional church.

It is ironic that Caponsacchi's only temptation to wrongdoing comes through a distortion of his newfound sense of priesthood, and that this distortion comes, significantly, through the influence of the institutional church. The sin to which he is tempted and to which he temporarily falls victim is, surprisingly, a sin of omission. Nothing seems more out of character for this spontaneous man whom even the lax fellow-canon, his friend Conti, recognized as a man of action and a born hero. Conti, Guido's cousin, fearing the Count's "feline teeth" too much to risk aiding and abetting his wife, nevertheless signals the proper knight to rescue her:

> 'Our Caponsacchi, he's your true Saint George—
> To slay the monster, set the Princess free,
> And have the whole High-Altar to himself.'
> (VII, 1323-5)

Nothing could demonstrate more acutely than Caponsacchi's inaction the powerful influence of the material church on the young priest, and just how inimical this influence is to his realization of both priesthood and selfhood. After pledging his help to Pompilia, he procrastinates for two nights, thereby inflicting terrible suffering on one he had decided to serve:

> I looked up, saw the sunset: vespers rang:
> She counts the minutes till I keep my word
> And come and say all is ready.
> (VI, 1027-9)

Left to itself, Caponsacchi's troubled mind is invaded by the church's long-lived, well-developed teaching on women, its insinuating formula now directed toward Pompilia: "This is a fleshly woman" (VI, 981). She who had appeared to his own perception as a Raphael madonna, "Our Lady of All the Sorrows," whose need had defined his own priesthood, has become, by the church's insinuation, "a fleshly woman," temptation's self. The church that had tarnished, at its inception, Caponsacchi's sense of priesthood, and given him an unworthy ministry, now tries and almost succeeds in turning the new missionary away from his newfound sense of purpose, precisely through its traditional portrayal of women.

The old dictum of woman-as-sin did not seem to apply when Caponsacchi, as a young priest, was given the ministry to flatter and amuse rich women benefactors by his music, his charm, his poetry, and his good looks. Indeed, when he first turned from these foppish pursuits in the wake of seeing the madonna-like Pompilia, he was chided by his sacerdotal patron—

> 'Young man, can it be true
> That after all your promise of sound fruit,
> You have kept away from Countess young and old
> And gone play truant in the church all day long?
> (VI, 469-72)

—who, in turn, did not appreciate Caponsacchi's retort:

> 'Sir, what if I turned Christian? It might be.
> The fact is, I am troubled in my mind,
> Beset and pressed hard by some novel thoughts.'
> (VI, 474-6)

The church had encouraged him to disdain the praying monk Caponsacchi stumbled over at the altar-foot in his haste to answer the summons of "some foolish fan" (VI, 984). Now that the summons is to sacrifice clerical favor to rescue a wife imperiled body and soul, the church changes its tone:

> Now, when I found out first that life and death
> Are means to an end, that passion uses both,
> Indisputedly mistress of the man
> Whose form of worship is self-sacrifice—
> Now, from the stone lungs sighed the scannel voice
> 'Leave that live passion, come be dead with me!'
> (VI, 996-1001)

Even so, Caponsacchi obeys the scannel voice, betraying his own instinct—the instinct of a man and priest "Whose form of worship is self-sacrifice." He is deluded by false asceticism into thinking that the denial of this instinct would be a higher form of self-sacrifice, not perceiving whom he really would be sacrificing by his inaction. What goes on in his head during these two days of rationalizing procrastination, Caponsacchi is careful not to class as thought (VI, 937 ff). His hindsight sees clearly that

> . . . all the harm
> My folly had crouched to avoid, now proved a veil
> Hiding all gain my wisdom strove to grasp.
> (VI, 954-6)

Caponsacchi, the man of spontaneity, is paralyzed by the considerations of society and church and is grateful not to transgress them, thereby compromising Pompilia, and adding loss of reputation to her real sufferings. His impasse and false reprieve are a direct response to long conditioning:

> Thank God so far!
> I have saved her from a scandal, stopped the tongues
> Had broken else into a cackle and a hiss.
> (VI, 1050-3)

To his credit, Caponsacchi does not succumb to the old insinuation of woman-as-sin in Pompilia, or, as we find later on, in womankind. He has, rather, succumbed to the promptings of human respect, that poorly named quality which not only prizes appearance over reality, but, in its cynicism, is incapable of judging an innocent reality under a compromising appearance. Because he is dealing with a society and a church that judge woman as sin, the priest wants to shield her from their inevitable interpretation of her action. But, unwittingly, he is dealing on their terms. What he does not understand is that Pompilia already has turned her back on conventional societal values in the plan of action she has chosen. They mean nothing to her. She has moved into a world of freedom and responsibility on whose threshold he perilously teeters.

When, after two days' procrastination, Caponsacchi resolves to go to Pompilia, it is not to save her, but to give her worldly counsel:

> 'The plan is rash; the project desperate:
> In such a flight needs must I risk your life,
> Give food for falsehood, folly or mistake,
> Ground for your husband's rancour and revenge' —
> (VII, 1462-5)

His truth has been tarnished by his yielding to a line of reasoning he knows in his heart to be false. In using words not his own, Caponsacchi appears to Pompilia as "one star / Turning now red that was so white before" (VII, 1467-8). He is restored to truth as soon as Pompilia confronts him with her straightforward reprimand laced with an unanswerable question:

> 'Why is it you have suffered me to stay
> Breaking my heart two days more than was need?
> Why delay help, your own heart yearns to give?'
> (VI, 1065-7)

Caponsacchi's monologue (VI) immediately precedes Pompilia's (VII), and it is moving to see how her account charitably underplays the details of her two-days' anxiety while waiting for his return, whereas he details his procrastination with painful honesty. Amazingly, in spite of her previous experience with priests, Pompilia never loses faith in Caponsacchi's pledge. From the moment of his promise he becomes her star of Bethlehem. In her accounting she seems even to cut a whole day from his own version of the time the star kept her waiting:

> No pause in the leading and the light! I know,
> Next night there was a cloud came, and not he:
> But I prayed through the darkness till it broke
> And let him shine. The second night he came.
> (VII, 1458-61)

When Caponsacchi starts his speech of cautious protection, Pompilia intuitively sees beyond the words his true steadfast self, of which she has, as yet, no concrete experience:

> I felt that, the same loyalty . . .
> One service apprehended newly: just
> A word of mine and there the white was back!
> (VII, 1467, 69-70)

Once returned to his true self—the self that was reclaimed from the ashes of his training, that took shape under Pompilia's commission—Caponsacchi never wavers. Words that had tried to prevail during his struggle with pusillanimity seem now truly to define him: ". . . I am a priest. / Duty to God is duty to her. . . ." (VI, 1029-30). With Dantean insight he attributes his rectification to Pompilia: "I too have seen a lady and hold a grace" (VI, 1105). He sees his service to Guido's wife as the only truly priestly act of his short sacerdotal career. When he had first realized in his life "the gap 'twixt what is, what should be" (VI, 487), Caponsacchi's first thoughts of Pompilia were on how he, a priest, could save her:

Thinking moreover . . . oh, thinking if you like,
How utterly dissociated was I
A priest and celibate, from the sad strange wife
Of Guido. . . .
(VI, 491-4)

In the society and the church of seventeenth-century Italy, there is no way for this priest to save this victim of a rapacious and murderous marriage, simply because the brutal conditions of her bond are accepted as normal, "woman's proper lot." That Pompilia is Guido's property to be disposed with as he wills all society concurs. Pompilia is the first to break the deadly circuit of custom and form when she decides, first, not to consummate the marriage, and, finally, to leave her husband altogether. Only when she summons him to her does the priest find an outlet for all his strengths, lying unused but fortunately not atrophied. Pompilia fuses new life into Caponsacchi by giving him a mission; he in turn saves her life by rescuing her from Guido, for a little while and, ultimately forever.

Caponsacchi's delay, in large part, is due to his ignorance of the magnitude of Pompilia's peril. He could not know, having not been told the particulars of her married life, of the dangerous despair in her continuation of that life. Pompilia's experience of marriage has so dispirited her that she has given up on life itself, "Careless until, the cup is drained, I should die" (VII, 1203). Her only relief is the oblivion of sleep: "Done, another day! / How good to sleep and so get nearer death!" (VII, 1220-1). There could be no consolation, no healing in this frame of mind, for Pompilia inevitably slides deeper into despair until she contemplates suicide, a thought manifesting "The frightfulness of my despair in God" (VII, 1285). She feels further debased by a sense of personal sin in this response of self-destruction. When she experiences this ultimate despair the only hope for deliverance must come from outside herself. Being powerless and having exhausted every possible resource available to her, and having been turned down by those most knowledgeable of her peril, Pompilia is reduced to utter hopelessness. The realization of her pregnancy breaks into this nadir—she has someone else to live for. This moves her to seek help once more, but this time outside convention and law.

In a passage of extraordinary lyric beauty, Pompilia recounts the revelation of pregnancy breaking in on her life like a summons, a mandate to live and be happy:

> . . . What, first thing at daybreak, pierced the sleep
> With a summons to me? Up I sprang alive,
> Light in me, light without me, everywhere
> Change! A broad yellow sun-beam was let fall
> From heaven to earth,—a sudden drawbridge lay,
> Along which march a myriad merry notes,
> Mocking the flies that crossed them and recrossed
> In rival dance, companions new-born too.
> On the house-eaves, a dripping shay of weed
> Shook diamonds on each dull grey lattice-square,
> As first one, then another bird leapt by,
> And light was off, and lo was back again,
> Always with one voice,—where are two such joys?—
> The blessed building-sparrow! I stepped forth,
> Stood on the terrace,—o'er the roofs, such sky!
> My heart sang. . . .
> (VII, 1222-37)

The sense of life, in powerful syntactic juxtaposition to her death-wish, is expressed here in a renewed vision of reality. The beauty of the world, the purposeful life of its creatures, appropriately reflect her own renewed gift of life. Only with this experience does her own life once again become precious, her own to use as she wishes. Only with this renewed sense of self-value does she find the pragmatic and concrete courage to do something to preserve it. Her new vision is like a drawbridge over Guido's moat imprisoning her in his palace of gloom. She will find a way out:

> Now—see if I will touch an unripe fruit,
> And risk the health I want to have and use!
> Not to live, now, would be the wickedness,—
> For life means to make haste and go to Rome
> And leave Arezzo, leave all woes at once!—
> (VII, 1255-9)

Pompilia's resolution to leave Arezzo and all her woes is the great moment of choice transforming her from passive victim to responsible agent of action. Her new sense of purpose, moreover, gives her the courage to do an extraordinary thing—to ask a stranger to risk all to save her. There is no mistaking her knowledge of how costly such involvement would be for a priest. When Caponsacchi becomes impeded by his fears for what *she* would suffer from ostracism, she cuts short this line of argument, which long since could mean nothing to her. She clearly sees the precariousness of *his* position as a priest: " 'Tis yourself / Risk all, not I,—who let you. . . ." (VII, 1471-2). This is not the girl who grovelled at the feet of the Archbishop, who humbly sued for the protection of the Governor, or who, after confessing despair to Fra Romano, begged his modest assistance. This is a woman who, determined to save herself, has the generosity to understand and acknowledge the heroic magnanimity called for in her rescuer. The others she had asked for help represented power. Even the pious humble Romano represented spiritual authority, which yet he dared not use by going contrary to the powers over him. The sympathetic priest Conti feared to incur the wrath of his cousin the Count, backed as he was by Governor and Archbishop:

> 'Above my strength!
> Guido has claws that scratch, shows feline teeth;
> A formidabler foe than I dare fret:

> Give me a dog to deal with, twice the size!'
> (VII, 1314-7)

Pompilia can guess the opprobrium reserved for a priest going blatantly contrary to such a power structure. Yet she asks the twenty-four-year-old canon to lay his manhood and his priesthood on the line to save her and this new life which she has no power to save, only the resolution. Her request is not selfish arrogance nor thoughtless presumption, but an act of hope and trust in Caponsacchi's courage and goodness as a priest dedicated to service.

Pompilia's trust in Caponsacchi is entirely intuitive.[4] She had seen him only once in the theater when Conti had drawn her attention to his companion by throwing "a foolish twist of comfits into her lap," then taking cover behind Caponsacchi, so that when she looked to see who had flung them, Pompilia faced "This Caponsacchi, looking up in turn" (VII, 981). Instinctively she knew the flirtatious gesture was not his:

> Ere I could reason why, I felt sure,
> Whoever flung them, his was not the hand.
> (VII, 982-3)

His "earnest face" is contrasted with that of "Fat waggish Conti, friend of all the world" (987): "The other, silent, grave, / Solemn almost, saw me, as I saw him" (989-90). That the grammatically ambiguous last statement, ". . . saw me, as I saw him," surely indicates more than a statement of fact is borne out by all that follows in their tale, and which will be discussed in the next chapter. Each seems to see the true person beyond either the levity or the menace of circumstances: Conti crouching playfully behind Caponsacchi to put his companion in a compromising position; Guido crouching sinisterly behind Pompilia to spy out a possible entrapment of his wife. Guido, for his part, pounces upon the opportunity thus provided:

'You are a wanton, — I a dupe, you think?
O Christ, what hinders that I kill her quick?'
Whereat he drew his sword and feigned a thrust.
(VII, 1328-30)

Thus begins Guido's elaborate plot with forged letters of seduction
from Caponsacchi, using his servant-mistress Margherita, his wife's
maid, as provocateur and go-between. "Broken-in to bear," Pompilia
increasingly resorts to sleep as a means of relief. Under Margherita's
insistent urging of a rendezvous with the priest, she becomes increasingly withdrawn, only occasionally prodded into a retort: "I know /
All you report of Caponsacchi false, / Folly and dreaming" (1179-81).
The reason for her faith in him against her maid's insinuation is based
on her one sight of the priest in the theater:

The face I fronted that one first, last time:
He would belie it by such words and thoughts.
Therefore while you profess to show him me,
I ever see his own face. Get you gone!
(VII, 1183-6)

Her faith in the truth of Caponsacchi's face is not shaken, but, under
the constant association of his name with her supposed seduction,
Pompilia recoils from the name, if not the reality behind it:

That name had got to take a half-grotesque
Half-ominous, wholly enigmatic sense,
Like any bye-word, broken bit of song
Born with a meaning, changed mouth and mouth
That mix it in a sneer or smile, as chance
Bids, till now it means nought but ugliness
And perhaps shame.
(VII, 1329-35)

In her newfound purpose and resolution Pompilia has no possibility of rescue except from Caponsacchi, recommended by Conti as a born hero-saint, but associated by Guido's intrigue with designs of seduction. Under such circumstances her willingness to risk all on his truth is an extraordinary act of faith and resolution. Ironically, considering Caponsacchi's hitherto superficial way of life, Pompilia has implicit faith in his sense of priesthood. Indeed, notwithstanding her crushing disappointment in Fra Romano, she retains a steadfast faith in priesthood itself, saying to Conti, "Carry me off! What frightens you, a priest?" (VII, 1313). Driven to this new and unknown source for help, she has only the recommendation of the worldly and cowardly Conti to go on—"he's your true Saint George"—and his assurance that all the rumors about Caponsacchi's wish to proposition Guido's wife are "pure birth of the brain" with no foundation in truth. These words of assurance from Conti, nevertheless, combine with her own intuitive faith in Caponsacchi. His imminent journey to Rome provides her with one possibility of escape, and she will reach for it, realizing it is "Not the man, but the name of him, thus made / Into a mockery and disgrace" by insinuation and gossip. She sees Caponsacchi as the priesthood's one true representative in her world, and, using Margherita's intrigue as a ruse, summons the priest to her. This is an extraordinary action based on an extraordinary faith and reliance on his capacity to see her action in its true light.

Pompilia's radical decisions do not stop with her resolve to leave her husband. When she is dying, the young mother claims sole parenthood for her son Gaetano. Having been conceived through her husband's hatred and saved only by her love, Pompilia claims for herself the sole life-giving role:

> My babe nor was, nor is, nor yet shall be
> Count Guido Franceschini's child at all—
> Only his mother's, born of love not hate!
> (VII, 1762-4)

With inexorable finality she unfathers Guido: he has no right to the fruit of her womb because he acted in a lie at the child's conception. Indeed, had not the unborn life been saved through her determination and Caponsacchi's courage, the child would never have been born:

> Yes, he saved my babe:
> It would not have peeped forth, the bird-like thing,
> Through that Arezzo noise and trouble: back
> Had it returned nor ever let me see!
> But the sweet peace cured all, and let me live
> And give my bird the life among the leaves
> God meant him!
> (VII, 1656-62)

Pompilia's is a singular position, clearsighted and discerning. A natural repugnance for the offspring of such a forced union might well be a mother's response. But Guido cannot seem to tarnish her maternal joy. She wrests it from his grasp. The young woman can love the child as her offspring, the child of her love, her tenderness. She can enjoy the fact of having given life to another human being without the taint of her husband. The fact is that she has efficaciously gone beyond him: he can no longer touch her. By an inexorable logic Pompilia divorces Guido, just as she unfathers him. She lays the divorce at his door: he accomplished the dissolution of the marriage by the twenty-two murder wounds he inflicted on her with his Genoese dagger:

> . . . Whereas strange fate
> Mockingly styled him husband and me wife,
> Himself this way at least pronounced divorce,
> Blotted the marriage-bond: this blood of mine
> Flies forth exultingly at any door,
> Washes the parchment white, and thanks the blow.
> (VII, 1713-8)

Having been brought up in a milieu where divorce was not named and not even thinkable, Pompilia can pronounce these words with a complete and awesome moral authority and relief. In her summation of their marital union and its outcome, Pompilia expresses gratitude for a kind of radical purgation brought about through the agency of her husband's final act of hatred:

> His soul has never lain beside my soul;
> But for the unresisting body, — thanks!
> He burned the garment spotted by the flesh!
> Whatever he touched is rightly ruined: plague
> Is caught, and disinfection it has craved
> Still but for Guido; I am saved through him
> So as by fire; to him — thanks and farewell!
> (VII, 1733-9)

The gratitude here is not stated with cheap irony, though it is power-fully ironic that a wife could be grateful for a husband's inevitable murder of her. Pompilia's sense of debasement and hopeless despair, inflicted by Guido during four years of marital contamination, is a much deeper injury to her selfhood. His touch ruined her with an in-eradicable plague that craved disinfection. She sees death, his final act of violation, as just such purgation. By it she is divorced from his in-fection completely, delivered at last from both Guido's lingering pol-lution and all fear of further contamination, and can pronounce the terrible valediction: "We shall not meet in this world nor the next" (VII, 1719). As long as both lived, Pompilia would never be securely beyond the contaminating reach of his hatred:

> And as my presence was importunate, —
> My earthly good, temptation and a snare, —
> Nothing about me but drew somehow down
> His hate upon me, — somewhat so excused
> Therefore, since hate was the truth of him.
> (VII, 1723-7)

Just as there is nothing of convention in Pompilia's other choices—her abandonment of her husband, her refutation of his paternity, her dissolution of the matrimonial bond—her forgiveness also takes an original form. Her words of eternal dismissal of Guido—"We shall not meet in this world nor the next"—are not words of damnation, and are followed by a curious benediction:

> But where will God be absent? In His face
> Is light, but in His shadow healing too:
> Let Guido touch the shadow and be healed!
> (VII, 1720-2)

Too honest to claim any desire for union with Guido in another life anymore than she would in this, she is, nevertheless, too charitable, too unarrogant to presume to pronounce another's damnation. This wife who can say unobtrusively, "I could not love him, but his mother did" (VII, 1731), can realize that God mysteriously might still cure Guido of his evil. She judges the evil unequivocally, but amazingly refrains from final judgment on its agent. Her forgiveness of this man is not a mealy-mouthed conventionally pious posturing for the benefit of her auditors. At Castelnuovo she had seen Guido as the "master, by hell's right" (1586), "the serpent towering and triumphant" (1589), "that ice-block 'twixt the sun and me" (1595), "the neutralizer of all good and truth" (1596)—all satanic images. Her assessment of him has not changed; she is simply beyond the need of worrying about his retribution.

Unlike the cynical world which judges Pompilia and Caponsacchi's escape as an adulterous elopement, Pope Innocent (Book X) praises the two deviants as the only representatives of truth in a world incapable of apprehending goodness: "What does this world, told truth, but lie the more?" (X, 672). His analysis of that world which conspired to destroy Pompilia is detailed, thorough, incisive, and devastating. The documents before him, bearing the various testimonies in Guido Franceschini's murder trial, are to him

> . . . this filthy rags of speech, this coil
> Of statement, comment, query, and response,
> Tatters all too contaminate for use. . . .
> (X, 372-4)

Unlike the lawyers who rely on nothing but their ability to manipulate words in order to distort the truth, the Pope considers that "barren words / . . . more than any deed, characterize / Man as made subject to a curse" (X, 348-50). Yet he knows "these dismalest of documents" (X, 213) contain the truth. His task is to discern it:

> Truth, nowhere, lies yet everywhere in these—
> Not absolutely in a portion, yet
> Evolvable from the whole: evolved at least
> Painfully, held tenaciously by me.
> (X, 228-31)

As Pope, he is asked to pardon Count Guido Franceschini *pro honoris causa*. As a man Antonio Pignatelli—"My ancient self, who wast no Pope so long" (383)—he will answer for his judgment. Quaintly he asks the *man*—"The one whose speech I somewhat trust" (394)—to judge the words and actions of the *pope*. Immediately one sees in this man the sense of self-direction and personal responsibility that marks Pompilia and Caponsacchi as his spiritual kin. Knowing "it is the seed of act / God holds appraising" (271-2), he will judge the deeds surrounding this murder trial by the quality of their intents, not by the dictates of a patriarchy whose misogynistic base he discerns quite clearly. All his judgments are completely contrary to the values flaunted by his culture and its "relics of routine" (1999).

Nowhere in *The Ring and the Book* is the culture and its history so strikingly analyzed and so unequivocally condemned as in the Pope's soliloquy. That no audience is present dramatically and artistically strengthens the aura of moral authority around an old man who knows this might well be the last act of his life. Like Pompilia, he speaks from the brink of death. Clearly he sees a culture that produced a wife-murderer like Guido and now pleads his cause—husband's honor—in a crime so cowardly, so cruel, and blatantly premeditated. He is, moreover, ruefully aware of the role the church has played in maintaining this society,

> Whereof the main prop was, is, and shall prove
> —Supremacy of husband over wife!
> (X, 2034-5)

Upholding the prop is the main function of custom, the law, and the church. He hears society's answer to any disputation of man's authority as absolute and unquestionable:

> 'And there's but one short way to end the coil,—
> By giving right and reason steadily
> To the man and master: then the wife submits.'
> (X, 2042-4)

The Pope disagrees. He sees the devalued Pompilia as the most valuable person in his society; Guido, the least. She is "first of the first, ... perfect in whiteness" (X, 1003, 5). With all her limited capacities, advantages, and education, she is crowned and armed like a preeminent angel; she is "earth's flower" (1017) in the untoward ground. Guido, on the contrary, having been born, nurtured, and educated with every advantage, is a rust that festers blight and corruption:

> For I find this black mark impinge the man,
> That he believes in just the vile of life.
> (X, 510-1)

Pompilia foils this quality to corrupt by her innate integrity:

> Here the blot's blanched
> By God's gift of purity of soul
> That will not take pollution, ermine-like

Armed from dishonour by its own soft snow.
(X, 676-9)

The Pope singles out the specifically feminine capacities of Pompilia — "mother, wife, and girl" — and makes a salient and unusual assessment of them: "Which three gifts seem to make an angel up" (X, 1951, 52). In the history of patriarchy only the first of these has been valued. As to Guido, "Not one permissable impulse moves the man" (X, 536), and Pompilia's assessment of her husband is corroborated in every estimation by the pontiff. He sees the marriage itself as a trap and a pretense:

A marriage — undertaken in God's face
With all those lies so opposite God's truth,
For ends so other than man's end.
(X, 569-71)

He articulates how society defines a wife's role as her husband's "slave, his chattel, to use and then destroy" (X, 564).

Continually the Pope probes beneath pretense and prevarication to expose the truth of the heart, and give it its proper language. Thus, he cuts through the Archbishop's rationalized noninterference with husband's privilege: "He needs some bone to mumble, help amuse / The darkness of his den with. . . ." (X, 1462-3). He summarizes the cowardice of the priest Romano as a callous and fully enlightened breach of faith: "I break my promise: let her break her heart!" (X, 1484). He sees betrayal and avarice in the Convertite nuns' attempt to cheat Gaetano out of his inheritance by reversing their testimony about his mother's character: "who was saint is whore" (X, 1522-3). In the latter case, he is particular to underscore the more odious betrayal by a community of women "that lives through helpfulness / To women for Christ's sake." This religious community was specifically founded to minister to women injured *as women* in a culture that devalues them. They are, in the Pope's words, "Meant to help women because these helped Christ" (X, 1499). As a Christian the Pope also calls attention here to the wholly benevolent role women played in the life of Christ. These nuns betray their ministry by playing into the legal and ecclesiastical system that can dispose of a murdered woman's inheritance solely on the testimony of men whose accusation is the insubstantial fabrication of adultery. The nun's testimony attempts to give substance to the man-made lie. The Convertites are creatures of the culture, daughters of patriarchy. What saddens the Pope as he probes for the "seeds of intent" among all the participants is the pervasiveness of resignation, acceptance, and complicity in cultural values known by the heart to be wrong. Pompilia and Caponsacchi alone are innocent of this complicity, and he celebrates their hearts' freedom.

Indeed, the Pope's own freedom of mind and heart is astounding in one who heads an institutional church long given to misogyny. In an interesting twist of a *Genesis* text (3:15), the Pope sees the once docile Pompilia rising, by her very disobedience, to a higher kind of law, not man's law, but God's. He praises her impatience with the law imposed by man, celebrating her as a woman prophesied by God's self—the woman who will crush the head of the serpent.[5] The Pope tells Pompilia to

> plant firm foot
> On neck of man, tread man into the hell
> Meet for him, and obey God all the more!
> (X, 1060-2)

One would be hard pressed to find in Western literature such a use of this text. No one but Browning's Pope has used *Genesis* to equate man with the serpent, thereby indicating man as lamia, man-as-sin, while manifesting woman as God's conqueror who will set things right by throwing off the yoke of man—"Sublime in new impatience with the foe" (X, 1059). Far from condemning Pompilia as an erring wife, Innocent praises her for her very rebellion, considering it obedience to a direct trumpet call from God "to the new service, not / To longer bear, but henceforth fight" (X, 1058). With particular verve he singles out for special praise Pompilia's sword-swinging threat of violence to her husband at Castelnuovo when the rabble pinioned Caponsacchi defenseless. To the Pope's original mind, she did in that act "Anticipate the office that is mine" (X, 1081) — the papal office! She was acting as the Pope's surrogate, brandishing a two-edged sword against her husband in defense of her rescuer. Clearly the Pope sees it as his duty to go contrary to the sacrosanct principle of *honoris causa* embodied in this killer husband. He likewise sees it his duty to defend the young priest whose conduct goes directly against the same principle. He praises Pompilia for executing his office in his absence. He does not hesitate thus to place this runaway wife at the highest level of a church which had not even granted her the privilege of living. With a further thrust of his logic he also dubs Caponsacchi as papal delegate, doing no less than the Pope's own duty in coming to the aid of this abused wife. For, to this man, the duty of the Pope as Christ's vicar is defined as the ministry of Christ's own choice: defending the powerless, relieving the oppressed. Such thinking is dramatically outside the structures of the church and the society operating in these proceedings. Most decidedly the Pope does not speak for Civilization.

Caponsacchi, in the Pope's estimation, is "less true" than Pompilia, "less practised in the right" (X, 1086), yet "surely not so very much apart" (X, 1094). Both are his spiritual children, and his affection comes through every line addressed to them, though the tone is appropriately different for each. Both seem to know the right path by instinct, not by cultivation. Their originality is therefore singular. The Pope muses on Caponsacchi's conduct, and with affectionate cajolery marks its source in a heart rightly oriented. The priest's action serves as an antimasque mocking the masque of culture and form:

> Here comes the first experimentalist
> In the new order of things, — he plays the priest;

Does he take inspiration from the Church,
Directly make her rule his law of life?
Not he: his own mere impulse guides the man.
(x, 1909-13)

In spite of bad training by the institutional church, this "Irregular noble scapegrace" turns into "my warrior-priest," "my athlete" leaping into the breach with

> . . . the chivalry
> That dares the right and disregards alike
> The yea and nay o' the world.
> (x, 1113-5)

Though the Pope praises Caponsacchi for his right action, he realizes that in another it could have gone amiss because of a defect in the heart. The efficacy of such action depends on the goodness and truth of the one performing it. Nor can the priest teach others to take the right step. It seems to depend on the quality of the person. Radical innocence comes with the habit of goodness — a habitual choice of the good. The only fault he finds with Caponsacchi in his rescue of Pompilia is his donning of secular dress which the Pope sees as "hypocrite's-disguise," "fool's-costume." He considers that, since Caponsacchi was performing a priestly function, he should have dressed as a priest, matching his clothes with his soul's truth:

> . . . which lie was least like truth,
> Which the ungainlier, more discordant garb
> With that symmetric soul inside my son,
> The churchman's or the worldling's, — let him judge,
> Our Adversary who enjoys the task!
> (x, 1133-7)

At first glance, it seems a small point, but upon reflection one sees portentous implications. Had Caponsacchi worn clerical garb, the

Castelnuovo incident might have failed for Guido. Perhaps the authority of his priesthood would have carried the day against Guido and his henchmen. Would the villagers have pinioned a priest to give sway to the slinking count? Had he protected Pompilia with the outward signs of his priestly authority, as well as its reality, perhaps he could have forestalled the accusations of adultery which his disguise reinforced. These are unanswerable speculations, but valid ones. The Pope's point of contention against Caponsacchi's dress surely brings them to mind. His point is, however, moral, not pragmatic. No matter what the reaction of others, one should do what one thinks is right, not disguising it in any way to accommodate cynical misinterpretation. The truly edifying act dilutes its efficacy by disguise. Caponsacchi therefore did well to lay his priesthood at the service of Pompilia; he did not do well to disguise this priestly ministry.

Of all Pope Innocent's strange and untoward tastes, his predilection for the poet Euripides indicates two culturally deviant orientations: one, an enlightened sympathy for women in a male-created, male-dominated culture; the other, an insight that the god adored by this culture is man's self, magnified to infinity. In his love and admiration for this particular Greek poet, Browning was a pioneer among Victorians. As Richard Dowgun points out in a recent volume of the *Browning Institute Studies*,[6] Euripides was held in generally low esteem during most of the nineteenth century. Schlegal's negative assessment dominated critical opinion, and not until after 1870 did the interest of Victorian critics turn to Euripides, seeing an analogy between the playwright's Athens and modern Europe. Just as Browning sees a message for his own age in the Franceschini murder case, so does his Pope see a lesson for seventeenth-century Rome in the works of Euripides.

Although the dialogue between the playwright and the Pope does not refer to any specific plays, a look at the plays and the fragments reveals an unremitting observation, analysis, and presentation of the suffering of women in a male culture. It is a world where a good wife like Alcestis is expected to give her life for her husband; a world where women are raped by gods and men; where Creusa and Phaedra despairingly exclaim over how deeply men hate women; where Jason and Hippolytus express this misogyny by wishing they could bear children without the aid of women; a world where the Trojan women are meted fates particularly humiliating to their womanhood: the holy virgin Cassandra to be the concubine of Agamemnon, the queenly Hecuba to be the slave of Odysseus—the man she most despises among her conquerors. It is a world divided, as Philip Vellacott points out, into "two separate worlds living side by side: the world of free males, and the world of women and slaves."[7] In such a world, quite simply, a man's life is more valuable than a woman's. According to Vellacott, Euripides "presents the position of woman as being, even in the most-favored circumstances, ultimately precarious and dependent on the will, the good opinion, and the activities of man."[8] The world that crushed Pompilia bears a striking resemblance to the one presented by Euripides.

One utterance from the plays seems particularly relevant to the institution of marriage as experienced by Pompilia Comparini. Nowhere in the literature of antiquity is the plight of women so clearly articulated as in one of Medea's speeches decrying the cultural imperative to marriage, and the virtual impossibility of human intercourse in that institution:

                                Oh,
Of all things upon earth that bleed and grow,
A herb most bruised is woman. We must pay
Our store of gold, hoarded for that one day,
To buy us some man's love; and lo, they bring
A master of our flesh! There comes the sting
Of the whole shame. And then the jeopardy,

For good or ill, what shall the master be;
Reject she cannot; and if he but stays
His suit, 'tis shame on all that woman's days.
So thrown amid new laws, new places, why
'Tis magic she must have, or prophecy—
Home never taught her that—how best to guide
Toward peace this thing that sleepeth at her side.
And she who, laboring long, shall find some way
Whereby her lord may bear with her, nor fray
His yoke too fiercely, blessed is the breath
That woman draws! Else, let her pray for death.
(—*MEDEA*, 230-48)[9]

In every line one can trace the plight of Pompilia Comparini, who was sold into a marriage so destructive she sought her own death.

In his fantasized encounter with Euripides, the Pope, as the representative of Christianity, is taken to task about its subservience to a flawed god made in man's image and paid the homage necessary to maintain that image. Euripides, unsatisfied with the cruel philandering Zeus, exposes his evil as evil, "nor swerved the more from branding brow / Because the sinner was called Zeus and God" (X, 1721-2). The behavior of gods should bear scrutiny, not blind imitation: ". . . what gods do, man may criticise, / Applaud, condemn" (X, 1746-7). In other words, Euripides' questioning of the gods' morality is an example which Pope Innocent will imitate. He looks at the god created by his culture and recognizes the image of man's creating. The god is in turn applauded for making man in *his* image, making man the master, giving him a disposable servant and chattel—his helpmate, woman. Guido knows this god well. His whole defense is based on that knowledge. Though he prefers Virgil's tempestuous Jove Aegiochus to the Christian deity, he knows well how to quote scripture to his purpose and to call upon that god to witness for him in upholding civilization, the *status quo*. All the teachers and scholars cited in Guido's defense have been honored in tradition, many of them rewarded with the conferral of sainthood by the church they served. Euripides chides the Pope for the church's long tradition of canonizing teachers of falsehood, who, in spite of the advantage of Christ's unique example, "miss the plain way in the blaze of noon" (X, 1784), whereas his own example and strong confrontation of truth, unenlightened as it was by Christianity, could have led these teachers out of

> That mire of cowardice and slush of lies
> Wherein I find them wallow in wide day.
> (X, 1788-9)

So much for the Pope's estimation of the church's magisterium, establishing man in God's image and woman in the image of sin. The most startlingly original thought of Browning's Pope Innocent is the need for revising the very concept of god-as-man into God as the transcendent mystery—the *Other* in whose image humankind, woman and man, was fashioned. To the Pope, God is "The central truth, Power, Wisdom, Goodness, — God" (X, 1633). The great need of culture and religion is to

> Correct the portrait by the living face,
> Man's God, by God's God in the mind of man.
> (X, 1872-3)

Until the concept of God is altered, man will go on in blind adoration of his masculine self with its concomitant denial of woman's value. Confirmation of self, in this guise, necessitates the elimination, the trivialization of the other. It depends on, rests upon the metaphysics of sexual inequality. Its god is man's self. Worship of such a god demands misogyny. To question this god is the radical core of Innocent's thinking, and this murder case has brought his thinking to articulation. The entire culture pleads for the pardon of Count Guido Franceschini for one reason: *honoris causa*. Man's honor is God's own, as Guido affirms by precept and example. In his first monologue the

Count threw down the gauntlet, "*Quis est pro Domino?*" (V, 1549) which Innocent now takes up: " 'Who is on the Lord's side?' asked the Count. / I, who write . . ." (X, 2100-1). Whoever is for the God of "Power, Wisdom, Goodness" must judge Count Guido Franceschini as a murderer. The Pope thus refuses to align himself with this murderer and the culture that nurtures him.

Only these three — Pompilia, Caponsacchi, and Pope Innocent — stand aside to judge the culture. Like Euripides they have adopted virtue as their rule of life, "Waived all reward, and loved for loving's sake" (X, 1711). They each possess what Browning calls "the triple soul" — strength, intelligence, and goodness — reflecting in their own limited ways the very qualities of God's self, the central truth of Power, Wisdom, and Goodness.

4 THE EQUILATERAL TRIANGLE

So we are made, such difference in minds!
Such difference too in eyes that see the minds!
(VII, 918-9)

                                           — a sense
That reads, as only such can read, the mark
God sets on woman, signifying so
She should — shall peradventure — be divine.
(VII, 1499-1501)

To learn not only by a comet's rush
But a rose's birth, — not by the grandeur, God —
But by the comfort, Christ.
(VII, 2094-6)

IN RESUSCITATING this Roman murder story from the Old Yellow Book, Browning infuses its sordid facts with a wonderful love story. Different readers, however, tend to wonder differently about it, as the body of literary criticism attests. The eyes of the cynical world of seventeenth-century Rome saw the relationship of Pompilia and Caponsacchi as plain sex adorned with the trappings of romance. The physical beauty of the pair reinforces this opinion, for, in the words of Bottinius, his main problem as Fisc is to show "How so much beauty is compatible / With so much innocence!" (IX, 765-6). Other luminaries in *The Ring and the Book* have identical opinions. The Other Half-Rome, though sympathetic to Pompilia, assesses Caponsacchi's testimony: "The tale here frankly outsoars faith: / There must be falsehood somewhere" (III, 906-7). He sees their story as "All extemporized / As in romance-books! Is that credible? (III, 921-2). When he notes that Pompilia and Caponsacchi "understood each other at first look" (III, 1063), he is using innuendo to say what the two *really* meant by their attestation of instantaneous intuitive faith in each other. Many readers from Thomas Carlyle[1] to the present would agree.

All depends on how one perceives and defines *love*. The worldling Tertium Quid pontificates that Caponsacchi came to the rescue of Pompilia, not for the altruistic reason he gives, but "for the natural end, the love of man / For woman whether love be virtue or vice" (IV, 994-5). For their declaration of motives, he sarcastically calls Pompilia and Caponsacchi "the pair of saints" (IV, 1044). The pornographically oriented Bottinius, in his superior sagacity, quips his deduction from the facts: Pompilia "was found to proffer nothing short of love / To the priest whose service was to save her" (IX, 508-9). For his authority he cites Venus's reward for service: "His be a supersweet makes kiss seem cold!" (IX, 534). Obviously to the Fisc love equals sexual intercourse. Guido, as one would expect, defines love as a courtly charade:

> . . . the beating pulse, the rolling eye,
> The frantic gesture, the devotion due
> From Thyrsis to Neaera! Guido's love—
> Why not provençal roses in his shoe,
> Plume to his cap, and trio of guitars
> At casement, with a bravo close behind?
> Good things all these are, clearly claimable
> When the fit price is paid the proper way.
> (V, 670-7)

The "fit price" for such arduously complimentary behavior is, of course, sexual favor. To Guido love has no place in marriage. As his property a wife is bound to whatever disposal her husband wishes to make of her; adultery, on the other hand, must be earned. Guido's concept of love is entirely acceptable to his auditors; Pompilia's is dismissed as incredible.

Both Caponsacchi and Pompilia have trouble with the word *love*. They see the snickers, winks, and nods that accompany the mention of it. They are *accused* of love. As the world defines it, love is an amusingly guilty thing which Caponsacchi refers to more severely as "The mundane love that's sin and scandal too" (VI, 130). It is clear they speak from two different worlds of moral perception. As to the forged letters used against him in court the canon labels them "a pack of stupid and impure / Banalities called letters about love— / Love indeed! . . ." (VI, 1651-3). He clearly sees such love as "Damnation pure and simple to her the wife / And me the priest" (VI, 1832-3). He fairly shouts at his judges, "I have done with being judged. / I stand here guiltless in thought, word and deed!" (VI, 1860-1). Unequivocally he repudiates the accusation of this kind of love. It has no part in him:

> . . . As for love, — no!
> If you let buzz a vulgar fly like that
> About your brains, as if I loved, forsooth,
> Indeed, Sirs, you do wrong! We had no thought
> Of such infatuation, she and I. . . .
> (VI, 1969-73)

The climax of Caponsacchi's struggle of repudiation comes in the long passage where he wishes punishment for Guido (VI, 1887-1954). Vigorously the priest condemns Guido, not to death, but to a distended hell of loneliness and isolation in a world that now knows him for the wife-rapist and wife-killer he is. He envisions Guido as sliding out of life, pushed by the general horror and common hate until he reaches hell itself, where his ultimate punishment will be union with Judas in a grotesque parody of the mundane love he so swaggeringly celebrated in life:

> The two are as one now! Let them love their love
> That bites and claws like hate, or hate their hate
> That mops and mows and makes as it were love!
> (VI, 1938-40)

Betrayal masks a reality of hatred with an appearance of love. Judas betrayed Christ with the kiss of friendship, discipleship; Guido betrayed Pompilia through the trappings of marriage, the sign of spiritual union. To Caponsacchi it seems fitting that he, who degraded his wife in marriage by an act which the world calls love before murdering her in outright hatred, should be punished by this curious ritual equating love and hate.

Pompilia, herself untouched by the least shade of sexual cynicism, is unfeignedly surprised to see how universal is the foregone conclusion of her adultery. She is shocked that people so readily believe untruths:

> Do only hear, it is the priest they mean,
> Giuseppe Caponsacchi: a priest — love,
> And love me! Well, yet people think he did.
> I am married, he has taken priestly vows,
> They know that, and yet go on, say, the same,
> 'Yes, how he loves you!' 'That was love'— they say
> When anything is answered that they ask:
> Or else 'No wonder you love him'— they say.
> (VII, 163-70)

Her amazement is based not only in her lack of cynicism, but even more so in her sense of personal integrity. To Pompilia it is inconceivable that anyone would expect her to unselve herself. Since her value system precludes the performance of acts contrary to their meaning, she, a wife, and Caponsacchi, a priest, will never be united physically, nor do they wish to be. Thus she sees the futility of Guido's intrigue to shame her in deed,

> To make me and my friend unself ourselves,
> Be other man and woman than we are.
> (VII, 707-8)

Many times during her monologue Pompilia rejects the word *love* in its popular usage. She makes neither linguistic nor moral mistake about the sexual solicitations of Guido's youngest brother, Girolamo. She names them a "soliciting to shame called love" (VII, 844), and declares that this "idle priest" taught her

> what depraved and misnamed love
> Means, and what outward signs denote the sin,
> For he solicits me and says he loves. . . .
> (VII, 810-2)

She refers to her sexual experience with Guido as "what hate calls love" (VII, 876), and in their Castelnuovo confrontation dismisses her husband as a "love-making devil."

The fact that Browning has both Pompilia and Caponsacchi spend so much thought and so many words on this problem of linguistic connotation is significant. That the poet has the rest of the world articulate its own idea of love with such cynical clarity, and downright obscenity, provides the reader with a base to measure the extent to which these two principals stand apart from that world and its values. Browning's characterizations of Pompilia and Caponsacchi within the framework of their culture constitutes a moral chiaroscuro. Pompilia reflects upon this contrast and articulates it with clarity:

> So we are made, such difference in minds,
> Such difference too in eyes that see the minds.
> (VII, 918-9)

Perhaps there is no more conceptually imprecise word in English than *love*, and none more prone to misinterpretation. One must always define what one means by it, never able to count on a mutual understanding between speaker and listener. We translate the Greek *eros* and *agape*, the Latin *amor* and *caritas* into one word, *love*, though the concepts are so different. Because of its pejorative connotation as one of the seven deadly sins, we have virtually expunged the word *lust* from linguistic usage and replaced it with *love*, thereby increasing our confusion. The word *lovers* in current usage has come to mean, exclusively, those who, regardless of personal attachment, engage together in sexual intercourse. So exclusive and entrenched has this usage become that in a court of law it has no other meaning. Though we have retained the word *eros* the concept is totally unfocused, people applying the expression with culpably ignorant abandon to pornography, torture, and the murder and dismemberment of women. A glance at the film advertising page of any newspaper bears this out. Again, though we have retained the Latin word *caritas* in the English *charity*, the word in English usage most frequently applies to any odious self-serving largess to the "deserving poor." So confusing conceptually is the word *love* that T.S. Eliot, when concluding *The Waste*

Land (1922) with the climactic message of salvation—the directive to unselfish love—put the words in Sanskrit, thus dramatically indicating how foreign is the very concept of *agape* or *caritas* to the culture.[2] The problem of connotation has always existed, and Robert Browning, the Victorian poet, has no trouble seeing the familiar symptoms in every testimony of the seventeenth-century murder trial. To Browning, having gone to great pains to saturate *The Ring and the Book* with manifestations, delineations, definitions of self-gratifying mundane love, he renounces it through the characters of Pompilia, Caponsacchi, and the Pope. Through them he redefines *love* as he understands it, thus freeing himself to use it as he wills. For Browning true love, whether in the frame of sexuality, family, or friendship, is the love of *agape* or *caritas*—unselfish, unpossessive, responsible love issuing from goodness. He celebrates this love with buoyant joy.

Once more we can look to Browning's Pope for the poet's definition. Innocent equates love with goodness, and he frequently interchanges the two words. God's image, he says, is reflected in humankind by its strength, intelligence, and goodness. But whereas humanity reflects adequately the first two qualities, it is deficient in the last, thus distorting God's perfect symmetry into an isosceles triangle. Goodness, the base that supports and shapes strength and intelligence, is inadequate in "The mass of men, whose very souls even now / Seem to need recreating" (X, 1892-3). Innocent contemplates the divine quality of goodness manifest to the world through the unspeakable generosity of the Incarnation—

> Thy transcendent act
> Beside which even the creation fades
> Into a puny exercise of power.
> (X, 1338-40)

To him the tale of the Incarnation supplies humankind with "love without a limit" (X, 1368). The benevolence manifested there is a love specifically "Unlimited in self-sacrifice" (X, 1370). Love is the outward movement of goodness. What the Pope sees as the undernourished, uncultivated quality in humankind is the unselfish, altruistic, unpossessive, and extravagant love taught by God's self. It is the love for which we have no adequate word—the love of *caritas*, the love of *agape*. Innocent celebrates the epiphany of this love in his world in the persons of Pompilia and Caponsacchi—"my rose," "my warrior-priest."

In his intriguing core passage (X, 1285-1659) the Pope, addressing God, refers to the Incarnation as "a tale of Thee / In the world's mouth which I find credible" (1347-8). Repeatedly he returns to the significance of "this tale" which "shows God complete" because it shows God as good. Since the actual tale before the Pope is Pompilia's, and her tale seems to have provoked his meditation, the reader is led into making a parallel between her story and that of the Incarnation. And, indeed, Pompilia has already set up this parallel in her monologue (VII), feeling herself caught up in an Incarnational drama, seeing its significance in her newfound life and happiness because goodness has touched her life so near the end. Recounting her fortnight of bliss surrounding the birth of her son at Christmas time, Pompilia tells of her newfound insight on the significance of the Incarnation. It accords with that of the Pope:

> I never realized God's birth before—
> How he grew likest God in being born.
> (VII, 1689-92)

Like the Pope, she sees love manifest in the Christmas story. From the moment Caponsacchi consents to take her away from Guido, Pompilia sees her whole drama as an intervention of God's loving kindness to save her life: first, through the revelation of her pregnancy, giving her a motive to live; and then, through the magnanimity of Caponsacchi, providing her with the means for escape. Thus the priest becomes her star of Bethlehem leading her to the "House of the Babe" whose saving mission she sees mirrored in her own child, Gaetano, whose annunciation gives her back her own life. She feels like Mary giving birth to her savior. Pompilia feels caught up in the drama through which divine love broke into the world. God's steadfast love has similarly broken into her world in the experience of being gratuitously loved and saved and restored to happiness by this priest. In a complex concatenation of ideas Pompilia describes the progress of her salvation and the roles played by her unborn child and her priestly rescuer:

> . . . My babe to be,
> That knew me first and thus made me know him,
> That had his right to life and claim on mine,
> And would not let me die till he was born,
> But pricked me at the heart to save us both,
> Saying 'Have you the will? Leave God the way!'
> And the way was Caponsacchi—'mine' thank God!
> He was mine, he is mine, he will be mine.
> (VII, 1450-7)

The heartpiercing joy of this last line is unmistakable. The echoic nature of the line reinforces the sense of the eternal nature of her relationship with Caponsacchi, for it reverberates from her remembrance of the priest's first words to her—"an eternity / Of speech to match the immeasurable depths / O' the soul that then broke silence—'I am yours' " (VII, 1447).

That Pompilia and Caponsacchi love each other there can be no doubt. Each, moreover, loves the other as a woman and a man. Each celebrates the peculiarly feminine or masculine qualities of the other. They are complementary, and each one blossoms in a complementary mutuality. Caponsacchi's masculinity, blatantly misdirected by the institutional church, finds specifically masculine fulfillment in helping

Pompilia, who has been rendered beyond societal help by reason of her very womanhood. Pompilia's femininity, bartered in the marriage market and devalued by her husband, finds womanly joy in the way she is treated by this man. The language, the images in which each describes the other are full of a lyrical extravagance that nevertheless rings sincere. To Caponsacchi, Pompilia is "The glory of life, the beauty of the world, / The splendor of heaven" (VII, 118-9). She is a saint, a "perfect soul" (VI, 1162) to whom his priestly audience will someday build churches. To Pompilia, Caponsacchi is white light blazing forth truth in every action (VII, 921). He is "a lustrous and pellucid soul" (VII, 935), "my angel" (1587) to whom she cries from her deathbed, "O lover of my life, O soldier-saint!" (VII, 1786). He is indeed a hero, a Saint George. Just the utterance of his name gives her strength. He is quite literally the one who loved her life enough to save it. When Caponsacchi waited for Pompilia between midnight and dawn on the night of her escape, he stood

> With a tune in the ears, low leading up to loud,
> A light in the eyes, faint that would soon be flare. . . .
> (VI, 113-34)

The crescendo of sound and light will be the arrival of Pompilia whose approach he sees in a climax of light and spiritual beauty. It is no ordinary coming

>   . . . at last,
> When the ecstatic minute must bring birth,
> Began a whiteness in the distance, waxed
> Whiter and whiter, near grew and more near,
> Till it was she: there did Pompilia come.
> (VI, 1137-41)

Pompilia, dressed in black from head to foot, he sees as white, her soul shining through the dark apparel. When she glides into the carriage, he perceives it as a cloud gathering up the moon (1145-6). This is not the ordinary way of perception. It is the perception of someone in love.

The only time they had ever spent together was the two-days' journey from Arezzo to Castelnuovo, twelve hours short of their destination in Rome. To Pompilia the entire journey was "one milky way" (VII, 1566) because of the comfort Caponsacchi wove around her. The details show a surpassing delicacy and intuitive understanding of her state both mental and physical. Pompilia had much reason to fear, much cause for depression. She recounts how, when evening passed into night her soul would sink, and how Caponsacchi could divine her thoughts and the surge of bitterness carrying her back to Arezzo to relive her torment through memory. He would then distract her by stories of the place they were passing, until she regained her courage. At one time when Pompilia was overcome with paralyzing fear, Caponsacchi sought out women, asking them to "Comfort her as you women understand!" (VI, 1326). Placing her in the company of women at the time of her pregnancy was the kindest thing he could have done, yet, even so, Caponsacchi seems to have surpassed himself, for Pompilia gives us further details of his consideration toward her: "Did not he find, bring, put into my arms, / A newborn babe?" (VII, 1555-6). He left her alone with these women whose talk of motherhood was the only womanly exchange she had had since her pregnancy dawned. The quality of Caponsacchi's love manifested in this action is not only considerate, but humble as well, admitting his own limitations as a man. His action is far from that of the possessive lover, jealously wishing to serve every need by his own resources, making self the moon and the stars of another. Indeed, Caponsacchi cites this unpossessiveness as a defense against his alleged infatuation, and points out examples of this quality in his conduct during the journey. He singles out how, at a little road-side place, he spent a good half-hour away from her "just to leave her free awhile" (VI, 1977). His pacing back and forth in the garden aimlessly plucking herb and bloom indicates his wish to be sitting beside her on the bench, but his consideration for her holds fast. One sees here the agitation of a man who loves and the magnanimity that puts the other's needs above his own. This whole passage of his monologue is moving because Caponsacchi, knowing Pompilia to be dead, now regrets the loss of that precious half-hour he could have spent with her. *Amor* and *caritas* are wedded—*caritas* completely informing *amor* in this man. Another point that takes on great significance, especially in view of what is revealed in discussions of painting by Guido and Bottinius, is Caponsacchi's description of Pompilia's beautiful face as one that painters would not approve. Caponsacchi's love can be traced clearly through his remembrance of every line and contour of her face, yet the reason hers is a face unacceptable for artists is that her brow seems crowned with "an invisible crown / Of martyr and saint" (VI, 1991-2), while the expression on her lips is "Careful for a whole world of sin and pain" (VI, 1996). In Guido-Bottinius parlance it is a Fra Angelico face radiating a deep inner life, not a Titian with its vacuous aura of gaudy flesh. She is not an art object, a piece of property. She is a living woman.

Near the end of Caponsacchi's address to the court, after he has made his mark upon them to the point of drawing tears from his auditors, he thrusts home: "You see the truth— / I am glad I helped you: she helped me just so" (VI, 1884-5). Just as he can trace his change of life to the first wordless moment he saw Pompilia, so now in the carriage journey Pompilia, by her innocent questions, provokes in the priest a renewed repudiation of his previous style as a canon. Her questions are intermittent, breaking unexpectedly and abruptly into the silence, thus indicating her sustained preoccupation with her rescuer. Pompilia, experiencing this wonderful care and exquisite consideration from Caponsacchi, sees such ministry as the very core of his life. She sees him specifically as a helper of women, but in so different a way from the charade of his first assignment at the Pieve. When she finds that his mother died at his birth and that he had no sister, she innocently asks what women he was used to serving before she called him away. He does not like the question for it reminds him only too well of the fribble and coxcomb years of his early priesthood. Another thing he does not like is Pompilia's surprise at his not reading the prayers at the ringing of the *angelus*. Both questions, however unwittingly, are pricks to his awakened conscience. Caponsacchi is rewarded when, in answer to his announcement that the "terrible journey" will soon be at an end, Pompilia says straightforwardly, ". . . If it might but last! Always, my life-long, thus to journey still!" (VI, 1311-2). The face and the voice of Guido haunt and terrify her; she feels safe with Caponsacchi to dispel her phantoms. But it is not just reliance on his strength and protection. Her words show the special intuitive knowledge of one who loves. She compares Caponsacchi's voice and his face to those of her dreadful husband:

> 'Yours is no voice; you speak when you are dumb;
> Nor face, I see it in the dark. I want
> No face nor voice that change and grow unkind.'
> (VI, 1316-8)

Her words express heart's knowledge and intuitive trust in the unalterable quality of his love. No wonder Caponsacchi's reaction, expressed eight months later in his testimony, is itself so natural and endearingly straightforward: "That I liked, that was the best thing she said" (VI, 1319). The line echoes those punctuating the two earlier questions so troublesome to the priest: Pompilia's query about his service to women — "I did not like that word" (VI, 1234); and the other about his punctuality to prayer — "I did not like that neither, but I read" (VI, 1274). His response each time shows a wry humor and a charming honesty of self-assessment, both enhanced by Browning's use of refrain-like repetition. By this small device the poet can bring out a quality not easily manifested in the horrifying situation of the novel. Most of Caponsacchi's humor—and there is much—is sardonic, directed as it is to the cynical church court itself or to the villainous husband and other actors in the evil drama.[3] But the journey with Pompilia, though fraught with fear of their being overtaken, is an idyll, a sharing in the mutual joy of reciprocal love and appreciation. The two times Pompilia asks the priest troublesome questions, he smiles at himself for having deserved by his previous folly the unease they afford.

These "best" words of Pompilia are a powerful declaration of love. To say she wishes the journey with Caponsacchi could last a lifetime, to say that she hears his words when he does not speak, sees his face in the dark indicate her love. The first time she sees Caponsacchi at the theatre, Pompilia, her marriage entering its fourth year of degradation, compares the priest to her husband and wonders, "Suppose that man had been instead of this!" (VII, 1007). For the first time she "learned there could be such a man" (VII, 949), and pictures what marriage to such a one would be:

> . . . Had there been a man like that,
> To lift me with his strength out of all strife
> Into the calm, how I could fly and rest!
> (VII, 998-1000)

These are speculations of an abused wife on what marriage could be under happier circumstances with the right partner. There is no concomitant desire for adultery.[4] Pompilia continually rejects the solicitations of Margherita to respond to the priest's alleged overtures. She continually affirms, moreover, her intuitive faith in Caponsacchi's innocence. The face she saw but once attests to his innate truth. There is no reason not to take her at her word. The character Browning created never speaks falsely, and speaks more simply than anyone else in the novel.[5] Caponsacchi also has reflected on what marriage to Pompilia would be. Only at the very end of his monologue—after the judges' faith in Pompilia is assured—does the priest reveal that he has played with "an imagined life," a life "companioned" by her:

> To live, and see her learn, and learn by her,
> Out of the low obscure and petty world—
> Or only see one purpose and one will
> Evolve themselves i' the world, change wrong to right:
> To have to do with nothing but the true,
> The good, the eternal—and these, not alone
> In the main current of the general life,
> But small experiences of every day,
> Concerns of the particular hearth and home.
> (VI, 2085-90)

Caponsacchi's concept of marriage as a life of mutuality where wife and husband learn each from the other, sharing thus their respective strengths and limitations, is a view not learned from either scripture or tradition. In a culture where men have no limitations and women are defined by them, there can be no mutuality between the sexes such as Caponsacchi has experienced with Pompilia and in terms of which he defines marriage. To him such marriage would be incarnational—each partner sharing, reflecting, imparting to the other the love of God experienced through the comfort of Christ: the down-to-earth manifestations of a love reflecting God's own mysterious love, steadfast and generous. But marriage with Pompilia is not his destiny in life. It is heartrendingly "far away"—a "mere delectation, meet for a minute's dream!" (VI, 2097).

Pompilia, whose first thought on seeing Caponsacchi was of marriage, and who knows unequivocally it is not in their destiny, gives, in her final reflections, some profound insights on the nature of marriage and vocation. Of Caponsacchi she says: "He is a priest; / He cannot marry, which is right" (VII, 1821-2). But she adds an intriguing thought, in view of Caponsacchi's anguish at losing her: "I think he would not marry if he could" (VII, 1823). To her marriage on earth seems a counterfeit, "Mere imitation of the inimitable" (VII, 1825). She cannot dissociate marriage from its institutionalization. Society, with its bartering of humans for goods and power, is incapable of nurturing or even believing in a reality of mutual love. No mutuality is possible, moreover, in a society that consistently and on principle devalues one of the partners, or in a church that has defined women as not in God's image, and where women are *given* in marriage, father to husband. She sees the real concept of marriage—wholeness through complementarity—fulfilled only in heaven. It is salvation. Reflecting on one of Christ's teachings on marriage, Pompilia comments:

> In heaven we have the real and true and sure.
> 'T is there they neither marry nor are given
> In marriage but are as the angels: right,
> Oh how right that is, how like Jesus Christ
> To say that!
> (VII, 1826-30)

Her citation from Mark's gospel (12:18-27) gives an account of Christ's answer to the Sadducees who, not believing in the resurrection of bodies, had concocted a theoretical and coarsely farcical case of a widow "left" in turn, as the law of Moses prescribed, as wife to seven short-lived brothers. To which would she "belong" in the next life, since all seven "had her?" Cutting through the pedantry as well as the cynicism, Christ made the comment cited by Pompilia about neither marrying nor being given in marriage. There is no need for the symbol of union and wholeness when its reality is secured through salvation. To Pompilia, being like the angels is completely human: "they are man and wife at once / When the true time is: here we have to wait / Not too long, neither!" (VII, 1836-8). Perfect union is more than physical; it encompasses what Shakespeare referred to as "the marriage of true minds" (Sonnet CXVI). To her, death will admit no impediment to such union, and in Pompilia's interpretation of Christ's teaching here, Browning goes far beyond the general popular idea of androgyny. In her vision the rift, the lack of understanding between the sexes experienced so destructively in her marriage and emanating from everything in her culture—that rift will be closed forever through such unions as herself and Caponsacchi. She has experienced this wholeness in her spiritual union with Caponsacchi, which, in her firm conviction, will never end. It is a salvation attained in spite of her culture's snares. And it was a costly purchase—akin to what T.S. Eliot described as "a condition of complete simplicity (costing not less than everything)."[6]

Pompilia, on the brink of death, has a sense of eternity to be spent inseparably with Caponsacchi. One sees the effect of this union in her present happiness and she speaks with an absolute authority about the future:

> 'T is now, when I am most upon the move,
> I feel for what I verily find—again
> The face, again the eyes, again, through all,
> The heart and the immeasurable love
> Of my one friend, my only, all my own. . . .
> (VII, 1771-80)

This friend indeed saved her life by giving her the only true happiness which she will have forever. Thus, with sincerity, and with no trace of false consolation, she can assure Caponsacchi that his mission of rescue was not a failure. He came to her aid to remove her from her evil husband and restore her to happiness. Both ends are accomplished irrevocably and the resulting happiness will not stop for death. The death consequent on her leaving Guido also has given her eternal deliverance not only from a marriage but from an association leading to personal damnation. Caponsacchi, who brought about her salvation, will never be separated from her in the communion of saints. She wishes him to know what she knows with unwavering certainty:

No work begun, shall ever pause for death!
Love will be helpful to me more and more
I' the coming course, the new path I must tread,
My weak hand in thy strong hand, strong for that!
(VII, 1788-90)

Again, in the last line Pompilia shows her sense of mutuality: the one rescued strengthens the rescuer and receives strength in return. Only such equality could produce the kind of understanding Pompilia shows for the plight of the priest. With the exquisite compassion of friendship Pompilia knows that her fate "Will have been hard even for him to bear" (1799), strong as he is. Her extraordinary sense of his presence, now and forever, gives her the understanding that this act of rescue, no matter the dreadful temporal outcome, was not in vain. She realizes that for him, a priest, saving her life was like her saving Gaetano — a life-preserving imperative. He indeed saved her life from lingering contamination, saved it for eternity. For the priest, to think of losing this life which he cherished would be a terrible fate; she insists, on the contrary, that she is not lost to him:

Ever with Caponsacchi! Otherwise
Here alone would be failure, loss to me —
How much more loss to him, with life debarred
From giving life, love locked from love's display,
the day-star stopped its task that makes night morn.
(VII, 1781-5)

Pompilia has no way of knowing, no way of hearing the last cry of Caponsacchi faced with the thought of a long life on earth without her: "O great, just, good God! Miserable me!" (VI, 2105); but she knows it with her heart, and with her last breath come words of understanding, compassion and encouragement for him to "wait God's instant men call years." Attributing her own salvation to Caponsacchi's intervention, her last directive to her auditors is to look to such exemplars for their own salvation, for only through such persons does God, stooping down, illuminate the darkness of the human heart so it can rise.

Like Pompilia, the Pope understands the terrible sense of loss for Caponsacchi. Innocent himself has come to love Pompilia, but will not long be separated from her. Like Pericles, the old Pope discovers a daughter in old age, and he will follow her soon into a new life. From the perspective and spiritual clarity of imminent death, he also has an unshakeable sense of the eternal and indestructible bond of his new-found love of this courageous young woman. But Caponsacchi is young and strong and will live a long time without Pompilia. It is as if the Pope too understands the last words of Giuseppe Caponsacchi's testimony. Though his faith in the priest's innocence is instantaneous and absolute, the Pope is in no way naive about human anguish. Radical innocence is never an untried state. Innocent is a wise man experienced in the problems of the human heart. Caponsacchi, with his symmetric soul, is not one of the isosceles triangles of this world. Yet the Pope realizes how intensely powerful are the priest's feelings for the woman he risked all to save. He seems to answer intuitively Caponsacchi's challenge to the court that priests "should study passion; how else cure mankind, / Who come for help in passionate extremes?" (VI, 2088-9), for the old Pope, pondering Caponsacchi's drama, asks the young priest if

> At any fateful moment of the strange
> Adventure, the strong passion of that strait,
> Fear and surprise, may have revealed too much,
> As when a thundrous midnight, with black air
> That burns, rain-drops that blister, breaks a spell
> Draws out the excessive virtue of some sheathed
> Sheet unsuspected flower that hoards and hides
> Immensity of sweetness, — so, perchance,
> Might the surprise and fear release too much

The perfect beauty of the body and soul
Thou savedst in thy passion for God's sake,
He who is Pity: was the trial sore?
Temptation sharp?
(X, 1171-83)

The intensity of his language here, the powerful lyricism in the sharp contrast of the night-lightning and flower metaphor, heightened by his dramatic use of a split chiasmus—such language manifests the piercingly tender quality of Innocent's perception of Caponsacchi's trial. The young priest is a hero, a Saint George who leads temptation like "reluctant dragons" by the head and hair. He does not avoid the battle with Guido's evil because of personal danger as did the other priests who turned away from Pompilia's plea for help. But never does the Pope minimize the personal pain brought by the priest's heroism. His valediction to Caponsacchi shows his understanding of the lifelong wound to be endured in an alien world without Pompilia's presence: "Once more / Work, be unhappy but bear life, my son!" (X, 1210-1).

In view of the cultural misogyny in *The Ring and the Book*, the love of Pompilia and Caponsacchi is outstanding in its mutuality and complementariness. Pompilia instantly senses the special masculinity of the priest, reflected poignantly in her paraphrase of Psalm 55, thinking if there were such a man as Caponsacchi to lift her out of all the strife, how she could fly and rest (VII, 998-1000). The psalmist is exclaiming on the rest found in the steadfast love of God. Pompilia obviously sees Caponsacchi as a manifestation of that love, a reflection of God's image—a symmetry of strength, intelligence, and goodness. Such an image is besmirched out of all recognition in the other men of her experience—Guido, the Archbishop, and the Governor. What is singularly extraordinary, however, is Caponsacchi's view of womankind which Pompilia sees reflected in every aspect and quality of the priest. In a church that from Saint Paul onward—from virtually its inception

— developed the separate definition theory of woman as not in God's image, this priest sees as the real nature of woman to be a reflection of the divine. Pompilia from her deathbed admonishes all men to take and sift her thoughts, calling attention to how different from the rest of his sex is Caponsacchi, "who from his own soul, re-writes / The obliterated character" (VII, 1504-5):

> — a sense
> That reads, as only such can read, the mark
> God sets on woman, signifying so
> She should—shall peradventure—be divine. . . .
> (VII, 1498-1501)

Caponsacchi's definition of woman as a reflection of God's image is the most startlingly untraditional formulation of this poem, which is set in a culture that defined women as, at best, expendable pawns and, at worst, disposable chattel. Pompilia remonstrates, moreover, that in straightening out this faulty definition of woman Caponsacchi used his love and strength to mend what was marred. Unmistakably she is pointing out that man abused his intelligence in making such a definition of woman, thereby implying that the misuse of intelligence is directly due to man's deficiency in love and strength. When the history of the separate definition theory is reviewed an unimaginable violation of the principle of charity (the very hallmark of Christianity) and a shocking debasement of logic is revealed in a legion of luminaries crowned for their labors with the halo of sainthood by a grateful church. No wonder Pompilia declares Caponsacchi a real saint. And there is a rapier-thrust in her explanation. Begging indulgence for her own ignorance in not having been privileged to see those whom the church called saints of old, she notes that she is but a soul in the bud "starved by ignorance" and "stunted to warmth." Is there any wonder that her discernment could be marred? How could such an undeveloped flower recognize the difference between the sun, the proper source of light and life, and "some insect with a heart / Worth floods of lazy music, spendthrift joy" (VII, 1519-21) — an insect who gave her "lustre for the dark, / Comfort against the cold?" Would not the stunted bud call this brave and jaunty fire-fly her sun? Her conclusion to this parable is a devastating indictment of orthodox, official sanctity, supposed to illuminate by the power of its example:

> What did the sun to hinder while harsh hands
> Petal by petal, crude and colorless,
> Tore me? This one heart brought me all the Spring!
> (VII, 1525-7)

Pompilia and Caponsacchi each considers the other as a saint precisely because they experience solely from each other the love of *caritas*. In them alone does the poet's spokesman, Pope Innocent XII, see this love manifest in the world of Count Guido Franceschini's Arezzo and Rome. To him they reflect, in their own limited ways, the balance of strength, intelligence, and goodness Browning conceives as the divine image in which humankind is created. The triple soul—body, mind, and heart—given to all human beings and distorted by most through an underdevelopment of the heart, is in these two a symmetric soul. Their symmetry is based in the love of *caritas* which upholds and shapes the qualities of strength and intelligence. They are, in Browning's precise and eccentric imagery, like equilateral triangles in a world of isosceles distortions.

5 CONCLUSION: ROBERT BROWNING, VICTORIAN FEMINIST

How wonderfully you understand the woman's
  nature!
No not *wonderfully*—I retract the senseless
  adverb—
most comprehensibly.
JULIA WEDGWOOD

I never saw a *man* like Mr. Browning in my life.
WILSON

'Tell me, are men unhappy, in some kind
Of mere unhappiness at being men,
As women suffer, being womanish?
VII, 1235-7

I can't tell you how wonderfully subtle some
touches of Pompilia seem to me. I feel as if
they must be a real woman's words. The
speech about the *pain of womanliness* is to me a
wonderful revelation of apprehension of our
side of the question. . . .
JULIA WEDGWOOD

IN THE ESSAY accompanying his translation of the Old Yellow Book,[1] Charles W. Hodell notes that Robert Browning deliberately had created a problem for himself by inventing the love between Pompilia and Caponsacchi, which was in no way indicated in the turgid documents of his source and was particularly vulnerable to the misinterpretation of his readers. Their actions would have been easier to justify in the eyes of the world had the poet not taken so bold a leap of imagination. As Hodell points out, Browning differentiated between lust/love and spiritual love independent of lust—a distinction not frequently made in Western culture, and therefore not easily discernible to many readers. Hodell notes further that the depiction of such love "can be conceived only by a very high-minded and pure worshiper of woman."[2] That the culture does not foster a great number of these is attested in its body of theology, literature, and art, much of which is tainted by devaluation and trivialization of women— woman as decoration, the male-created woman. In this ambience equality and reciprocation are ruled out, rendering the attainment of *caritas* impossible in sexual love. Browning, facing such a milieu, redefines love in the persons of Pompilia and Caponsacchi, but after a hundred odd years he is still swimming against the current, and for *The Ring and the Book* the poet has been accused continually of untruth, unreality, and infidelity to his sources. Browning did not create this problem nor fall into its subsequent critical snares unwittingly. Every monologue in his novel reveals how completely aware he is of the sexual cynicism emanating from the core of a patriarchal society.

He forthrightly addresses these issues with their destructive effects on women, and exposes them to an equally patriarchal society in his own Victorian England, the society that produced such men as Edward Moulton-Barrett from whose domination he rescued Elizabeth. Indeed, while Browning was resuscitating the male-dominated milieu of seventeenth-century Italy, his esteemed contemporary, Coventry Patmore, could glibly write to edify a Victorian public with his enormously popular and highly acclaimed definition of woman's role in society: "Man must be pleased; but him to please / Is woman's pleasure."[3] The style is far removed, but does this pleasure-principle definition of woman differ at all from Guido's or Bottinius's or that of any of the other spokesmen for Civilization in Browning's poem? Patmore's smug platitude is precisely the rationalizing for the male myth that women enjoy whatever men do to them — the more brutally subjugating, the more enjoyable. It is the justification for sexual abuse, pornography, and rape. Browning dramatically exposes this long-lived fallacy through the words and attitudes of Guido Franceschini and his supporters. He exposes and rejects it through Pompilia Comparini, the woman who refuses to accept such a role as God-ordained because church-supported, and through the two men who agree with her refusal, the priest, Caponsacchi and the pope, Innocent XII. *The Ring and the Book* is not only a powerfully incisive feminist judgment on the androcentric mores of patriarchy, and on its concomitant subjugation of women; it goes farther, judging and rejecting as an idol the god made by man in man's image: the god who devised, upholds, and enforces the laws of men, and severely punishes those who question them. In honoring this idol, man worships himself and his institutions, not the transcendent God whose image he shares equally with woman. Of all the men in *The Ring and the Book* only Caponsacchi and the Pope seem to know this. It is Caponsacchi's lucid articulation of the divine vocation and destiny of women that so moved Pompilia's heart and lifted her from despair and degradation.

The culture depicted prides itself on its subjugation of women as fulfillment of a divine mandate. It is the largest single source of Guido's bravura as he weaves his defense of the ultimate disposal of his wife. Pompilia's reticence to explicate her victimization is not matched in Guido's own account of their connubial rites, his sexual debasement of her, and of the satisfaction it afforded him to provoke from his wife the posture and words of abjection. Relish, not reticence, marks his style:

> There was an end to springing out of bed,
> Praying me, with face buried on my feet,
> Be hindered of my pastime, — so an end
> To my rejoinder, 'What, on the ground at last?
> Vanquished in fight, a suppliant for life?
> What if I raise you? 'Ware the casting down
> When next you fight me!' Then, she lay there, mine:
> Now mine she is if I please wring her neck, —
> A moment of disquiet, working eyes,
> Protruding tongue, a long sigh, then no more—
> As if one killed the horse one could not ride!
> (XI, 1352-62)

The Count's lingering fantasy of choking his wife to death makes a vivid association, in his mind, of sexual intercourse and the woman's death at the hands of her husband as the ultimate sexual submission. This association is a staple of pornography. His closing simile—the pornographic image of woman as a horse to be bridled and ridden by man, a horse to be killed at the whim of man—appropriately links Guido's idea of marriage to the whole culture's insidious vocabulary of the marriage rite still with us. The *bride* is *given away* by her father to her new owner, the *groom* who will saddle her and do with her what he will. Guido's speeches powerfully and with relish reveal the ominous cynicism of words we take for granted, but he, never. And he is echoed everywhere in his world. Bottinius, preparing his defense of Pompilia, sees it as unthinkable that "heifer brave the hind":

> We seek not there should lapse the natural law,
> The proper piety to lord and king
> And husband: let the heifer bear the yoke!
> (IX, 251-4)

Guido's predilection for food imagery in delineating woman's relation to man is echoed violently in the Archbishop's coarse marriage instruction parable to Pompilia (VII, 820-42), but no less significantly in the Fisc's prosecution brief where he compares a wife to a "cup . . . with olent breast" lying in readiness for her husband to "quaff at" (IX, 313). Moving from simile to metaphor, Bottinius proceeds to elaborate the "bounty" a husband has purchased in a wife, and which belongs to him exclusively as master:

> Haste we to advertise him—charm of cheek,
> Luster of eye, allowance of the lip.
> All womanly componants in a spouse,
> These are no household-bread each stranger's bite
> Leaves by so much diminished for the mouth
> O' the master of the house at supper-time:
> But rather like a lump of spice they lie,
> Morsel of myrrh, which scents the neighborhood
> Yet greets its lord no lighter by a grain.
> Nay, even so, he shall be satisfied!
> (IX, 318-27)

Just so does Paul Gauguin, thirty years after the publication of Browning's novel, serve up the breasts of Tahitian women on a tray of mango fruits for the consumption of the male viewer.[4] Only one year before the publication of *The Ring and the Book*, Rhoda Broughton humorously portrayed a woman's choice of becoming purchased goods through marriage:

His arm is around my waist, and he is brushing my eyes and cheeks and brow with his somewhat bristly mustache as often as he feels inclined—for am I not his property? Has he not every right to kiss my face off if he chooses, to clasp me and hold me about in whatever manner he wills, for has he not bought me? For a pair of first class blue eyes warranted fast colour, for ditto super-fine red lips, for so many pounds of prime white flesh, he has paid a handsome price on the nail, without any haggling, and now if he may not test the worth of his purchase, poor man, he *is* hardly used![5]

The food metaphor is a staple of the man-as-consumer, woman-as-goods idea, and Browning exposes it repeatedly and with verve.

When Julia Wedgwood complained of the overwhelming vulgarity of Guido, Browning retorted that ". . . all great (conventionally great) Italians are coarse—showing their power in obliging you to accept their cynicism."[6] His clarifying qualification here is a typically Browningesque discrimination between appearance and reality. Surely Guido's coarseness—a tool of power promoting cynicism—is the poet-dramatist's method of revealing, through irony, a villain; whereas, the character's own intention is to manifest a hero, an exemplar *par excellence* of the culture.

How uncompromisingly Browning cuts through the myths of virilism, and how incisive is his perception of their pervasiveness in his own world of Victorian England! His exposure of the ugliness and injustice of patriarchy through the characters of his Roman murder story is selective, detailed, and powerful. What he selects and fleshes out with his detailed dramatic characterizations are hardly the common concerns of his society: wife-rape, wife-murder, and the kind of bonded virilism that could approve, perpetuate, and boast of such practices. In no way, however, does Browning perceive the situation he describes as isolated to the world of *The Ring and the Book*. As he passionately explains to the friend who refused to accept his perception of the evil of that world and its pervasiveness: "The worst is, I think myself dreadfully in the right, all the while, in everything: apart, of course, from my own incapacities of whatever kind, I think this *is* the world as it is and will be—*here* at least."[7] The italics are his own, clearly indicating the contemporary relevance of his vision of worldly evil in the Franceschini murder case. Society, as he reveals it, is the embodiment of that evil, and Guido Franceschini is its exemplar and spokesman. Of his villain Browning writes to the same objecting friend, ". . . there will be nobody to match Guido, whose wickedness does . . . or rather, by the end, *shall* . . . rise to the limit conceivable. . . ."[8] Once again, his emphasis signals for special observation Guido's final utterances in his second monologue. They are not only his last testament and last summation of self: Browning's selective shaping of Guido's dramatic posturing reveals as well what mentality creates or emerges into these violent acts against women. He demonstrates, through Guido's language, his story-telling, his jokes, his obscenity, his prurient taste in painting, and his ultimate lasciviously detailed fantasization of the male-created woman, the very metaphysics of the pornographic culture. And he states that *there* Guido manifests his wickedness "to the limit conceivable." Decidedly, Guido's estimation of woman damns him in Browning's moral judgment—an extraordinary stance either for seventeenth-century Italy or nineteenth-century England. He stands unflinchingly, one foot with Caponsacchi and the Pope, the other with his contemporary, John Stuart Mill.[9]

Robert Browning's Christianity is often referred to as unorthodox. If the term denotes someone not committed to the institutional church with all its related structures of patriarchal control and suppression, it accurately describes the poet. But Browning's commitment to Christianity, if not the church, cannot be gainsaid. The kernel of Christ's moral teaching is the commandment to love one's neighbor as oneself—the altruistic love of *caritas*. Consequently, in order for a person to be declared a saint by the Christian church, the single most important criterion is a life of heroic charity. Browning goes to the heart of institutional failure in *caritas* by having the pre-Christian poet Euripides chide Pope Innocent for heading an institution which rewards with canonization teachers who stumbled in the darkness in spite of the light shed by God's Incarnation. The particular teachers Browning selects to expose are those cited as authorities in the Franceschini trial to justify the supremacy of men over women. These authorities, by defining woman as not in God's image and man as the masterpiece of creation, the vicar of God's self, and specifically defining woman's role as one created for man's service, comfort, and pleasure, have justified and supported the system of sexual inequality so endemic to institutionalized religion. As men who denigrate woman as outside God's creation of humankind, these teachers are collectively and individually spreading darkness through a monumentally uncharitable misogyny incompatible with the law of Christ. The pagan Euripides, who had

> Adopted virtue as my rule of life,
> Waived all reward, and loved for loving's sake
> (X, 1710-1)

is appropriately shocked.

Since the focus of *The Ring and the Book* is on the victim, Browning thereby has created a perfect vehicle for examining the attitudes and traditions of an ascendantly male culture supported by the patriarchal church so opposed to the *caritas* enjoined by Christ. The poet's insights into this androcentric culture and its institutions, particularly marriage, exude from every page. One insight is particularly intriguing—Pompilia's final reflection and comment on Christ's response to the Sadducees' challenge concerning the woman who "was given" in turn, by levirate law, to seven brothers (Mark 12:18-27). Pompilia sees Jesus's response about there being no place in God's heaven for marrying nor being given in marriage as a liberating revelation: ". . . right / Oh how right that is, how like Jesus Christ / To say that!" (VII, 1828-30). This has been discussed already in regard to her whole evaluation of institutional marriage and her spiritual union with Caponsacchi (Chap. IV). More radically still, she infers from Christ's words that in God's world there is no place for patriarchal marriage at all. That Browning would conclude this on his own is no surprise after his perception, through Pompilia, of what patriarchal marriage entailed for women. That he would use the passage from Mark as illustrative proof is theologically staggering for 1868. The eminent scripture scholar and theologian Elizabeth Schüssler Fiorenza recently has interpreted this passage in just such light.[10] She notes that the Sadducees' question aimed only at the controversial issue of the resurrection of bodies; it *assumed* the uncontroversial necessity of patriarchal marriage to insure the property and name of the male line. Jesus did not engage in their question because he did not share its assumption. Schüssler Fiorenza explains: "Jesus' response states flatly that they are wrong. They do not know either the Scriptures or the power of God, because they do not recognize that 'in the world' of the living God patriarchal marriage does not exist either for men or for women."[11] Pompilia's joy in the resurrection is based on this very insight in the passage from Mark. It is her last reflection before death, Pompilia's final pronouncement. It is a remarkable statement for the liberation of women by God from the structures of men.

One critic has claimed: "In Browning's fictional universe man is saved or damned by his attitude to woman. And thus Browning reached his characters' central truth in the light of his own."[12] One sees this clearly as the moral fulcrum of *The Ring and the Book*. Browning places Pompilia in God's heaven at the end, but only two of his men could ever make it — the two who believe in her, love her, and help and vindicate her, respectively: Caponsacchi and Innocent. The world of men he sees — as it was, is, and will be — has few who value womankind. Browning is not in the mainstream. In his estimation of women he is with Dante.[13] The "Inferno" is almost exclusively populated by men, while the key figures in men's salvation are women, Mary and Beatrice. Humankind restored to prelapsarian innocence is represented by a woman, Mathilda, in the Earthly Paradise. Eve and Adam—humankind restored—are both in the highest circle of the "Paradiso," but Eve, higher than Adam, is sitting at the feet of Mary, smiling. Browning, who sees womankind in God's image, would have seen Eve as Dante did, not as Milton's simpering destructor of man, reminiscent of Tertullian and John Chrysostom. Perhaps he would find delight in Charlotte Brontë's Shirley, who takes Milton to task and restores Eve to womanly splendor: "Milton's Eve! Milton's Eve! . . . Milton tried to see the first woman but . . . he saw her not. . . . It was his cook that he saw. . . ."[14] Browning amply demonstrates his contempt for an androcentric culture which has placed women in the role of servant and chattel to men. But *The Ring and the Book* is more than an exposure and condemnation of civilization's time-honored misogyny. It is a celebration of womankind in the person of Pompilia.

Pompilia Comparini, who comes across the pages of the Old Yellow Book as an unfortunate, faceless victim, Browning has transformed into a brave, self-directed young woman. Chained by the helplessness society devised for wives, she seeks help from that society and finds none. Ultimately she finds her rescuer outside the structures. Pompilia flees her husband with the aid of a priest who, by all expectations, should have urged her to remain and accept "the proper lot of women." She loves Caponsacchi without desiring physical consummation—loves in a way that culturally redefines *love* as *caritas*. On her deathbed, she divorces and unfathers her husband because of the crimes he has committed against her. And, simultaneously with these clear-sighted and tough-minded judgments, Pompilia forgives her rapist-murderer. Pompilia is the mover. Arthur Symons recognized Pompilia as principal: ". . . She makes and unmakes the lives and characters of these around her. . . . She is the heroine, as neither Guido nor Caponsacchi can be called the hero."[15] She judges and rejects, without arrogance, the role society and the church have devised for her. From the fallen Eden of her world, "the untoward ground," she springs up as "earth's flower," "First of the first," "Perfect in whiteness." Pompilia is the new Eve breaking into "the new order of things." Browning's Pope assesses her as the one human being in his fallen world who most splendidly reflects the divine image:

> . . . see how this mere chance-sown, cleft-nursed seed,
> That sprang up by the wayside 'neath the foot
> Of the enemy, this breaks all into blaze,
> Spreads itself, one wide glory of desire
> To incorporate the whole great sun it loves
> From the inch-height whence it looks and longs! My flower,
> My rose, I gather for the breast of God.
> (x, 1040-6).

Praising her for her very rebellion and disobedience against a corrupt culture, the Pope canonizes Pompilia in his valediction: "Go past me / And get thy praise. . . ." (X, 1091-2).

Browning's Pompilia is a celebration of womanhood, the embodiment of womanly capability—the ability to remain oneself in spite of what the culture dictates. Pompilia is not the woman created by man. In his characterization of Pompilia Comparini Browning exposes and judges the misogyny under which Western Civilization groans, and celebrates the femininity capable of releasing an androcentric culture from its enslavement in narcissism. By being what she is, Pompilia restores to humankind that womanhood deprived of definition. Thus she embodies the promise and possibility for *risorgimento*, not only of woman, but of the whole human race as well. In *The Ring and the Book* Robert Browning reveals and champions womankind as a treasure misused and misprised. In this assessment of women, Browning deserves the exclamation of Wilson, Elizabeth's maid: "I never saw a *man* like Mr. Browning in my life."[16]

NOTES

Foreword: Apologia Pro Vita Sua

1   William Clyde De Vane, *A Browning Handbook* (New York: F.S. Crofts, 1935), p. 37.

2   The two volumes of Browning's manuscript of *The Ring and the Book* are in the manuscript collection of the British Library housed in the British Museum. References in this study are to Richard D. Altick's edition (New Haven: Yale University Press, 1971).

3   Roma King, *The Focusing Artifice: The Poetry of Robert Browning* (Athens, Ohio: Ohio University Press, 1968), 135.

4   Elvan Kintner, ed., *The Letters of Robert Browning and Elizabeth Barrett 1845-6*, 2 vols. (Cambridge, Mass.: Harvard University Press, 1969), 601-6.

5   Kintner, 607.

6   Betty Miller, *Robert Browning: A Portrait* (New York: Charles Scribner's Sons, 1952), 104.

7   Kintner, 605.

8   Miller, *Portrait*, 63.

9   Miller, *Portrait*, 167.

10 See Patricia Thompson, *George Sand and the Victorians: Her Influence and Reputation in Nineteenth-Century England* (New York: Columbia University Press, 1977) for a fine exploration of the relationship of Elizabeth Barrett with George Sand.

11 Betty Miller, ed., *Elizabeth Barrett to Miss Mitford: The Unpublished Letters of Elizabeth Barrett Barrett to Mary Russell Mitford* (London: John Murray, 1954), 227.

12 Miller, *Letters*, 225.

13 Kintner, 159.

14 Kintner, 150.

15 Kintner, 157-8.

16 Kintner, 399.

17 Kintner, 403-5.

18 Miller, *Portrait*, 123.

19 Kintner, 212-3.

20 William Clyde De Vane, *Browning's Parleyings: The Autobiography of a Mind*, 2nd ed. (New York: Russell & Russell, Inc., 1964), 167-212.

21 Miller, *Portrait*, 110-2.

22 Mrs. Sutherland Orr, *A Handbook to the Works of Robert Browning*, (London: George Bell & Sons, (1902), p. 21, n. A reproduction of this engraving is the frontispiece in Henry Charles Duffin's *Amphibian: A Reconsideration of Browning* (London: Bowes & Bowes, 1956).

23 See Philip Kelly & Betty A. Coley, *The Browning Collections: A Reconstruction with Other Memorabilia* (Winfield, KS: Wedgestone Press, 1984), 471-512.

24 Kintner, xxi-xliv. See also William Clyde De Vane, "The Virgin and the Dragon," *Yale Review* xxxvii (September 1947): 33-46. De Vane traces Browning's use of The Andromeda myth from Pauline to the *Parleying with Francis Furini*.

25 Kintner, 214.

26 Frederic G. Kenyon, ed., *The Letters of Elizabeth Barrett Browning*, 2 vols. (New York: Macmillan, 1897), 288.

27 Kintner, 1018.

28 Kintner, 956.

29 Flavia Alaya, "The Ring, the Rescue, & the *Risorgimento*: Reunifying the Brownings' Italy," *Browning Institute Studies* 5 (1978): 1-41.

30 Alaya, 25.

31 Dorothy Mermin, "Barrett Browning's Stories," *Browning Institute Studies* 13 (1985): 108.

32 Kintner, 74.

Chapter 1   Introduction: The Filthy Rags of Speech

1 The Old Yellow Book and Browning's ring are housed in the Browning Collection at Balliol College Library. A facsimile and translation of this primary source for Browning's poem can be found in "The Old Yellow Book, Source of Browning's *The Ring and the Book*, in complete Photo-Reproduction with Translation, Essay, and Notes by Charles W. Hodell,"

Carnegie Institution of Washington (Pub. No. 89), July 1908. The Lord Baltimore Press, Baltimore, MD, U.S.A. For a detailed account of the correct identification of Browning's ring, see A. N. Kincaid, "The Ring and the Scholars," *Browning Institute Studies* 8 (1980), 151-60, and the Editorial Notes in *The Complete Works of Robert Browning*, vol. VII, Roma A. King, Jr., ed. (Athens, Ohio: Ohio University Press).

2   What Browning referred to as his "murder-story" has continually defied generic definition. Henry James saw Browning's poem as an unsuccessful novel: "The Novel in *The Ring and the Book*," *Notes on Novelists with Some Other Notes* (New York: Charles Scribner's and Sons, 1916). For a discussion of the genre of this long poem, see Susan Blalock, "Browning's *The Ring and the Book*: 'A Novel Country,' " *Browning Institute Studies* 11 (1983) 39-50. I sometimes refer to the poem as a *verse-novel* or, simply, *novel*.

3   See Richard D. Altick and James F. Loucks II's excellent analysis of this maze in *Browning's Roman Murder Story: A Reading of "The Ring and the Book"* (Chicago and London: University of Chicago Press, 1968); and Park Honan, *Browning's Characters: A Study in Poetic Technique* (New Haven: Yale University Press, 1961).

4   The volume of disputation on the validity of Browning's ring metaphor is enormous, and, since it is not the purpose of the present study to pursue that argument, I will not recount the various positions of the many scholars who have taken sides for or against the poet's gold-alloy analogy for his creative method. For a serious review of various scholarly positions see Paul A. Cundiff, *Browning's Ring Metaphor and Truth* (Metuchen, N.J.: The Scarecrow Press, Inc., 1972).

5   Richard Curle, ed. *Robert Browning and Julia Wedgwood: A Broken Friendship as Revealed in Their Letters* (London: John Murray and Jonathan Cape, 1937), 166. See 152-207 for their correspondence on *The Ring and the Book*.

6   For valuable surveys of both contemporary and updated critical reception, see the following: Ezzat Abdulmajeed Khattab, *The Critical Reception of Browning's "The Ring and the Book": 1868-89 and 1951-68, Salzburg Studies in English Literature: Romantic Reassessment*, 66, Erwin Sturzl and James Hogg, eds. (Salzburg: Institut fur Englische Sprache und Literatur, Universitat Salzburg, 1977). William Clyde De Vane, *A Browning Handbook* (New York: Appleton-Century-Crofts, 1955) includes critical data to 1935. William O. Raymond brings the survey up to 1949 in his chapter "England and America, 1910-49" in *The Infinite Moment* (Toronto: University of Toronto Press, 1950), 193-231. See also Boyd Litzinger and Donald Smalley, eds. *Browning: The Critical Heritage* (New York: Barnes and Noble, 1970).

These editors excerpt significant reviews from 1868 to 1870 in their chapter on *The Ring and the Book*, 284-353.

7 H. Allingham and D. Rodford, eds. *William Allingham: a Diary* (London: Macmillan, 1907), 207.

8 *The Death of the Wife-Murdering Guido Franceschini, by Beheading* (A manuscript found in London in 1862 by one of Browning's acquaintances who sent it to him).

9 Browning actually offered the manuscript of the Old Yellow Book to several contemporaries who turned him down. Undoubtedly their versions would not have been the same as Browning's.

10 A. K. Cook, in his indispensable *A Commentary Upon Browning's "The Ring and the Book"* (London: Oxford University Press, 1920), includes several appendices citing differences between Browning's reconstruction and the data of his sources. In Appendix V, 290-300, Cook carefully delineates the discrepancies between Caponsacchi's and Pompilia's monologues and the depositions upon which they are based. The account discovered in The Royal Casanatense Library, Rome, 1900, was included in an appendix of W. H. Griffin and H. C. Minchin, *The Life of Robert Browning*, 3rd ed. (Methuen, 1938). William O. Raymond unearthed another document concerning the murder and its aftermath in the Armstrong Browning Collection at Baylor University, Texas. See also Beatrice Corrigan, trans., ed. *Curious Annals: New Documents Relating to Browning's Murder Story* (Toronto: University of Toronto Press, 1956).

Chapter 2   Honoris Causa: Misogyny in Church and Society

1 Aristotle, *Generation of Animals*, A. L. Peck, trans. (Cambridge, Mass.: Leob Classics, Harvard University Press, 1943), I, 113.

2 Athenaeus, *The Deipnosophists, or Banquet of the Learned*, C. D. Yonge, trans. (London: H. G. Bohn, 1854) 3 vols., III, 13, 910-11.

3 Dionysius of Halicarnassus, *The Roman Antiquities*, E. Cory, trans. (Cambridge, Mass.: Harvard University Press, 1927), I, 381.

4 Aulus Gellius, *The Attic Nights*, John C. Rolfe, trans. (Cambridge, Mass.: Harvard University Press, Loeb Classics, 1927), I, 323.

5 *Code of Justinian*, IX, ix, 30, in S. P. Scott, trans., *The Civil Law* (Cincinnati: The Central Trust Company, 1932), XV, 8.

6 Livy, *The History of Rome*, Lat. ed., C. Weissenborn and M. Müller (Leipzig: B. G. Teubneri, 1900), 34, 140. Quoted in Julia O'Faolain and Lauro Martines, eds. *Not in God's Image: Women in History* (London: Virago, 1979), 57.

7   Gaius, *The Institutes of Gaius*, I, in S. P. Scott, 97. For feminist comment on the great number of books and treatises written about women by men, see Christine de Pizan, *The Book of the City of Ladies* (1405), Earl Jeffrey Richards, trans. (New York: Persea Books, 1982), 364; and Virginia Woolf, *A Room of One's Own* (New York and London: Harcourt Brace Jovanovich, 1929), Chap. 2.

8   Paola da Certaldo, *Libro di buoni costumi*, A. Schiaffini, ed. (Florence: F. LeMonnier, 1945), 105-16, 126-8. Quoted in O'Faolain and Martines, 182.

9   Current Scholarship questions the authorship of two of the Pauline passages cited here. Though the authorship of *Galatians* and *First Corinthians* is thought to be indisputably Paul's, *First Timothy* is widely considered the work of a first-century disciple of the Apostle, and to this disciple also are attributed verses 34 and 35 of chapter 14 of Paul's *First Epistle to the Corinthians*. The official canon of Pauline epistles, however, is the same now as in Browning's time, and the poet, as well as the seventeenth-century Roman Church considered all the Pauline epistles as the direct teaching of the Apostle.

Cf. Hans Conzelmann, *1 Corinthians: A Commentary on the First Epistle to the Corinthians*, James W. Leitch, trans. (Philadelphia: Fortress Press, 1975). Martin Dibelius and Hans Conzelman, *The Pastoral Epistle: A Commentary on the Pastoral Epistles*, Phillip Buttolph and Adela Yarbro, trans. (Philadelphia: Fortress Press, 1972).

10   *Works of Chrysostom*, Homilies on Timothy, IX, in Select Library of Nicene Fathers, P. Schaff, ed., Oxford trans. (New York: Christian Literature Co., 1889), XIII, 436 ff.

11   St. Augustine, *Of the Work of Monks*, H. Browne, trans., in Select Library of Nicene Fathers (Buffalo: Christian Literature Co., 1887), III, 524.

12   St. Augustine, *On the Holy Trinity*, A. W. Haddan and W. G. T. Shedd, trans., in Select Library of Nicene Fathers (Buffalo: Christian Literature Co., 1887), III, 159.

13   *Corpus Iuris Canonici*, A. Friedberg, ed., 2 vols. (Leipzig: Bernhardi Tauchnitz, 1879-81), I, pt. II, C. 33, q. 5, c. 12, 13, 17, 18. Quoted in O'Faolain and Martines, 143.

14   St. Thomas Aquinas, *Summa Theologica*, Fathers of the English Dominican Province, trans., 22 vols. (London: Burns, Oats & Washbourne, 1921-32), IV, pt. I, quest. XCII, art. 1, 2; XCIII, 4.

15   Aquinas, Quest. XCIII, 4.

16   Ibid.

17 For a good examination of the Guido/God analogy, see Altick and Loucks II, *Browning's Roman Murder Story*.

18 Tertullian, *De Cultu Feminarum*, I, 1, in Migne, *Patrologia Latina* (Paris: Apud Garnieri Fratres, 1884), I, cols. 304-5. Quoted in O'Faolain and Martines, 145.

19 *The Writings of Clement of Alexandria*, W. Wilson, trans. in Ante-Nicene Christian Library, A. Roberts and J. Donaldson, eds. (Edinburgh: T & T Clark, 1867), IV, 209.

20 For a rare opposition to clerical misogyny see Agrippo Von Nettesheim who wrote in his treatise *On the Nobility and Excellence of Women* (1529):

> "Wishing to take on human nature in its lowest and most abject state, so as the more effectively by this humiliation to expiate the first man's pride and sinning, Jesus Christ chose the male sex as the most despicable, not the female, who is nobler and more regenerate than the male. Moreover, because the human species was driven to evil-doing more by the sin of man than that of woman, God wanted the sin to be expiated in the sex that had sinned, whereas He [sic] wanted the sex which had been taken by surprise and tricked to bring forth Him in whom sin was to be revenged."

Agrippa, *De nobilitate et praecellentia foeminei sexus declamatio* (Paris: Babuty, 1713), 57, quoted in Julia O'Faolain and Lauro Martines, eds., *Not in God's Image: Women in History* (London: Virago, 1979), 196.

21 Titian, "Venus of Urbino," 1538 (The Uffizi); "Tarquin and Lucretia," c. 1570 (Fitzwillim Museum, Cambridge). See the discussion of the latter in *The Genius of Venice 1500-1600*, Jane Martineau and Charles Hope, eds. (London: Weidenfeld and Nicolson), 229-30. For a lucid analysis of this phenomenon, see Rozsika Parker and Griselda Pollock, *Old Mistresses: Women, Art and Ideology* (New York: Pantheon Books, 1981), especially chap. 4, "Painted Ladies."

22 Susan Griffin, *Pornography and Silence* (London: The Women's Press, 1981), 44. See also Andrea Dworkin, *Pornography: Men Possessing Women* (London: *The Women's Press*, 1981), especially chap. 6, "Pornography" and chap. 7, "Whores."

23 Charlotte Brontë, *Villette* (London: Oxford University Press, 1978), chap. 19, "The Cleopatra."

24 Edouard Manet, "Olympia" 1863 (Paris: Musee D'Orsay).

25 The cynical irony of the church court that assigned Caponsacchi to exile in Civita Vecchia for alleged adultery is not lost on the priest as he notes his

penal assignment: to produce a travesty translation of *De Raptu Helenae*, a Greek poem about the rape of Helen written about A.D. 500 in Egypt.

26 For a dissenting opinion concerning the Pope as the authoritative voice, see William E. Buckler, *Poetry and Truth in Robert Browning's "The Ring and the Book"* (New York: NYU Press, 1985), chap. 8.

Chapter 3 The First Experimentalists

1 Richard Curle, 167.

2 Philip Drew, "A Note on the Lawyers" *VP*, 6 (1968), 300.

3 Jerome L. Wyant, "The Legal Episodes in *The Ring and the Book*," *VP*, 6 (1968), 318.

4 See Mary Rose Sullivan's *Browning Voices in "The Ring and the Book": A Study of Method and Meaning* (Toronto: University of Toronto Press, 1969) for a perceptive analysis of intuition as the basis of the spiritual kinship between Pompilia and Caponsacchi.

5 The Douay version (1609) translates the verse using a feminine pronoun: "I will put enmities between thee and the woman, and thy seed and her seed: *she* shall crush thy head, and thou shalt lie in wait for *her* heel" (italics mine). The authorized King James Version uses neuter followed by masculine.

    Roy Gridley, in his "Browning's Pompilia," *JEGP*, 67:64-83, 1968, sees in the Castelnuovo scene a gloss on *Revelations* 12:9 with Pompilia as the Virgin, Caponsacchi as St. Michael, and Guido as the dragon Satan.

6 Richard Dowgun, "Some Victorian Perceptions of Greek Tragedy," *Browning Institute Studies*, vol. 10, 1983, Gerhard Joseph, ed., 83.

7 Philip Vellacott, *Ironic Drama: A Study of Euripides' Method and Meaning* (Cambridge: Cambridge University Press, 1975), 104. See particularly his chapter "Woman," 82-126.

8 Vellacott, 126. Another fine discussion is an earlier one by A. W. Gonne, "The Position of Women in Athens," in *Essays in Greek History and Literature* (Oxford: Blackwell, 1937).

9 Euripides, *Medea and Other Plays*, Philip Vellacott, trans. (New York: Penguin Classics, 1971), 24.

Chapter 4 The Equilateral Triangle

1 *William Allingham: A Diary*, 207.

2 Ann P. Brady, *Lyricism in the Poetry of T. S. Eliot* (New York: Kennikat, 1979), chap. 3.

3   Judith Wilt explores the significance of "The Laughter of Caponsacchi," *VP* 18:337-57, 1980.

4   For a perceptive assessment of Pompilia's and Caponsacchi's respective thoughts on marriage and their rejection of its possibility for them, see Mary Rose Sullivan, *Browning's Voices in the Ring and the Book: A Study in Method and Meaning* (Toronto: University of Toronto Press, 1969), 99.

5   In any edition, there are fewer annotations accompanying Pompilia's monologue.

6   T. S. Eliot, "Little Gidding" V, *Four Quartets, The Complete Poems and Plays 1909-50* (New York: Harcourt Brace, 1952), 145.

Chapter 5   Robert Browning, Victorian Feminist

1   The Old Yellow Book: Source of Browning's *The Ring and the Book* in complete Photo-Reproduction with Translation, Essay, and Notes by Charles W. Hodell. Carnegie Institution of Washington (Pub. No. 89) July 1908 (Baltimore: The Lord Baltimore Press), 283-84.

2   Hodell, 284. See also Roma A. King, Jr. *The Bow and the Lyre: The Art of Robert Browning* (Ann Arbor: The University of Michigan Press, 1957), 136, for a discrimination of lust from love in Browning's poetry.

3   Coventry Patmore, *The Angel in the House* (London: George Bell & Son, 1885), 73.

4   Paul Gauguin, "Tahitian Women with Mango Fruits" 1899, (New York: Metropolitan Museum).

5   Rhoda Broughton, *Cometh Up as a Flower: An Autobiography* (London: 1867), 326. Quoted in Elaine Showalter, *A Literature of Their Own: British Women Novelists from Bronte to Lessing* (London: Virago, 1978), 174.

6   Richard Curle, 156.

7   Curle, 166.

8   Curle, 167.

9   As a member of parliament John Stuart Mill worked for women's suffrage. He published *The Subjection of Women* in 1869, the same year *The Ring and the Book* appeared. Browning, however, was not an advocate of women's suffrage.

10 Elizabeth Schüssler Fiorenza, *In Memory of Her: A Feminist Theological Reconstruction of Christian Origins* (New York: Crossroad, 1984), 121, 144-45.

11 *Ibid.*, 144.

12   Henri Talon, "*The Ring and the Book*: Truth and Fiction in Character-painting," *VP*, VI, 3-4, 1968, 353-65.

13   See J. E. Shaw's article " 'The Donna Angelicata' in *The Ring and the Book,*" *PMLA*, XLI (1926), 55-81. Shaw sees the poem as Browning's dramatic exposition of his theory of love, "which is the most important part of his philosophy, and this theory of love is fundamentally identical with that of Dante" (p. 73).

14   Charlotte Brontë, *Shirley* (Oxford: Oxford University Press, 1979), Vol. II, chap. VII, "Which the Genteel Reader is Recommended to Skip, Low Persons Being Here Introduced."

15   Arthur Symons, *An Introduction to The Study of Browning* (London: J. M. Dent, 1906), 152.

16   Betty Miller, *Robert Browning: A Portrait* (New York: Charles Scribner's Sons, 1952), 146.

INDEX

"Abt Vogler," 21

Adultery, 13, 14, 15, 17, 30, 31, 34, 60, 71, 87, 90, 94, 102-104, 113

Aeleanus, Claudius, 33

Agamemnon, 95

Agape, 105-106, 111

Agrippo von Nettessheim, 140n

Alaya, Flavia, 8, 136n

Alcestis, 95

Alexander VII, Pope, 56

Allingham, William, 138n, 141n

Altick, Richard D., 137n

"Andrea del Sarto," 6, 24

Androgyny, 116

Andromeda, 7, 8, 9

Anouilh, Jean, 24

Antigone, 15

Aquinas, St. Thomas, 40-41, 139n

Archangeli (character), 65, 66-67, 88

Archbishop (character), 14, 15, 48, 49-54, 62, 81, 90, 119, 128

Arezzo, 13, 15, 18, 19, 20, 46, 48, 53, 60, 71, 72, 81, 85, 110, 121

Aristotle, 33, 40, 138n

Art, 6-7, 20-22, 56, 57-58, 111, 128, 140n, 142n

Ashburton, Lady, 3

Athenaeus, 138n

Augustine, Saint, 38, 139n

Baldinucci, Filippo, 6

Balliol College, 1, 136n

Barrett, Edward Moulton, 1, 3, 4, 5, 8

Barrett Browning, Elizabeth, compared to Andromeda, 7-9; *Aurora Leigh*, 8; Robert Browning, opposition to, 2, 3, 9; capital punishment, 2; finances, 1; immodesty, accusation of, 4; Italian liberation, 8-9; Rescue myth, transformation of, 8, 9; George Sand, 3-6, 135n

Bianca (character), 58

Blalock, Susan, 137n

Bottinius (character), 6, 7, 17, 65, 67, 88, 101, 111, 121, 128

British Library, 135n, 136n

British Museum, 7, 135n

Bronte, Charlotte, 58, 133, 140n, 143n

Broughton, Rhoda, 128-29, 142n

Browning, Robert, 18, 19, 120-21; art, knowledge of, 6-7, as truth, 20-22; composition of *The Ring and the Book*, 18-25, 57; contradictions, admission to, 9; capital punishment, 2; Christianity, 130-31; domestic relations, 4-5;

feminism, 1, 125-134; financial dependence, 1; incompetence, 3, 8; law, attitude to, 63-67, 125; love, definition of, 105-106, 115; love letters, 2 *passim*; mother, relation to, 3; opportunism, 3; Perseus, 7-9; rescue theme, 8-9; Sand, George, 3-6; tyranny, attitude to, 4-6; women, attitude to, 125-34

Browning, Robert, senior, 1

Browning, Robert Widemann Barrett (Pen), 1, 3, 6-7

Browning, Sarah Ann Widemann, 3

Byron, *Don Juan*, 4

Canon Law (*Corpus Iuris Canonici*) 39-40, 149n

Caponsacchi (character), 2, 3, 9, 13, 14, 16, 17, 20, 22, 23, 25, 32, 36, 46, 54, 56, 63, 68-80, 87-98, 101-121, 125-26, 130, 132; definition of woman, 119-121; humor, 113; love of Pompilia, 23, 25, 101-121, 125; priesthood, sense of, 36, 68-80, 92-94; rescue, 68-85, 107-117, 129

Caravaggio, 7

Caritas, 25, 37, 73, 78, 105-106, 111, 120, 121, 125, 130, 133

Carlyle, Thomas, 22, 101, 138n

Cassandra, 95

Castelnuovo, 13, 20, 47, 87, 92, 110

Castrati, 40

Cato, Marcus, 34

Cavaliere Servente, 36

Central Truth, 97-98, 132

Certaldo, Paolo, 35

Christ, Jesus, 41, 49, 83, 90-92, 97, 103, 106-108, 114-16, 130-32

Chrysostom, St. John, 38, 133, 139n

Church, 35-42, 48-52, 59-61, 65, 66, 70-79, 89, 90-92, 93, 96-97, 113, 119-21, 125-34

Civita Vecchia, 13

Clement of Alexandria, 42, 140n

Coley, Betty A., 136n

Communion of Saints, 115-16

Comparini, the, 13, 19, 31, 42-43, 45

Conti (character), 74, 81-82, 84

Convertites, 90

Conzelmann, Hans, 139n

Cook, A. K., 138n

Corrigan, Beatrice, 138n

Creusa, 95

Cundiff, Paul A., 137n

Curle, Richard, 137n, 141n, 142n

Damnation, 3, 5, 14, 17, 19, 43, 59, 68, 87, 116, 130, 132

Dante, Alighieri, 78, 132-33

Decretum, The (1140), 39-40

De Vane, William Clyde, 6, 136n

Dibelius, Martin, 139n

Dionysius of Helicarnassus, 34, 138n

Divorce, 84-87, 116, 133

Don Celestine (character), 45

Dworkin, Andrea, 140n

Eliot, T. S., 105, 115, 142n

Eros, 105

Euripides, 94-97, 131, 141n

Eve, 16, 37-42, 133-34

Evil, 2, 3, 22, 33, 41, 45, 96, 113, 119, 129-30

Exorcism, 46, 59-60

Feminism, 1, 125-34

Forgiveness, 45, 87, 133

Fra Angelico, 58, 111
"Fra Lippo Lippi," 6, 21, 24
Franceschini, the, 19, 23, 43, 45, 54, 72
Gaetano (character), 14, 73-74, 80, 84-85, 107-108, 117
Gaius, The Institutes of, 35, 139n
Gaugin, Paul, 128, 142n
Gellius, Aulua, 138n
Genesis, 37-42, 54, 91-92, 141n
George, Saint, 19, 20, 74, 83-84, 93, 109, 119
Girolamo (character), 19, 51, 54, 104
God, 32, 37-42, 44, 45, 47, 48, 51, 52, 53, 54, 55, 72-73, 79, 85, 88-90, 96-98, 106-108, 114, 117, 118-121, 126, 131-33
Good, 22, 93, 97, 98, 106-107
Governor, the (character), 14, 15, 52-54, 62, 81, 119
Griffin, Susan, 58, 140n
Guido (character), 3, 5-6, 13, 15, 16, 17, 19, 20, 24, 25, 29-32, 35, 37, 42-62, 65, 66, 67, 69, 71, 82-87, 88-92, 119, 129-30; artistic taste, 6-7, 57-58; God the Father, as, 41, 61; language, 29-32; marriage, idea of, 29-32, 35, 37, 42, 43-62, 79, 103, 109, 127-28; marriage ideal, 58-60, 96; privilege of nobility, 17, 30, 42, 55-57, 60-61; rape, 42-47, 109, 127-28

Half-Rome (character), 16
Hecuba, 95
Hero, 9
Hatred, 29, 43-45, 48, 49, 50, 60, 84, 86, 95, 103-104
Hodell, Charles W., 125, 136n, 142n
Honoris Causa, 13-18, 29-62, 88, 89, 92, 98

Incarnation, 78, 106-108, 114, 131
Innocence, 15, 17, 67-68, 77, 91, 93, 106-108, 113, 118
Italian Liberation, 1, 8-9
Ireland, Home Rule, 1

James, Henry, 137n
Jameson, Anna, 3
Jove, Aegicochus, 96
Judas, 103
Justinian, The Code of, 34

Kelley, Philip, 136n
Kenyon, Frederic G., 136n
Kenyon, John, 4
Khattab, Ezzat Abdulmajeed, 137n
Kincaid, A. N., 137n
King, Roma, 2, 137n
Kintner, Elvan, 7, 135n, 136n

Law, 29-62, 65-67, 80, 88, 89, 91-92
Leighton, Sir Frederic, 6-7
Lex Julia, 34
Litzinger, Boyd, 137n
Livy, 34-35, 138n
London University, 1
Loucks, James F., II, 137n
Love, 23-25, 31, 47, 49, 73, 84, 85, 87, 95, 101-21, 125, 133-34
Lucifer, 16
Lucrezia Borgia, 59-60
Lust, 38-39, 44, 45, 58-60, 105, 125

Manet, Edouard, 58, 141n
Margherita (character), 83-84, 113
Marriage, 3, 4-6, 13-17, 19, 25, 29-37, 42-62, 65, 72, 74, 79, 85-86, 88, 89-90, 91, 95-96, 98, 102, 109, 113-16, 131-32; wife-killing, 13, 15, 17, 32-35, 89, 92, 129; vocabulary of, 127-29

Mary, Virgin, 57, 69, 75, 107-108, 133
Medea, 95-96
Mermin, Dorothy, 8, 136n
Michael, Saint, 141n
Mill, John Stuart, 130, 142n
Miller, Betty, 135n, 136n, 142n
Milton, John, 133
Misogyny, 29-62, 89, 91, 97, 119-121, 131-34
Mitford, Mary Russell, 4
Motherhood, 53, 80-81, 84-85, 87, 90, 107, 110
"My Last Duchess," 5, 6

Odysseus, 95
Old Yellow Book, 15, 18, 20, 23, 24, 34, 101, 125, 133, 136n, 137n, 142n
Orr, Mrs. Sutherland, 7, 136n
Other Half-Rome (character), 16-17, 101
Oxford University, 1

Pandora, 42
Paolo, Abate (character), 19, 36, 49
"Parleying with Francis Furini," 6
Patmore, Coventry, 126, 142n
Patriarchy, 3, 6, 7-8, 13, 17, 29-62, 87-97, 94-98, 120-134
Paul, Saint, 37-38, 119, 139n
Pauline, 7, 9
Perseus, 7, 8, 9
Philomen, 34
Pietro (character), 42
Pignatelli, Antonio, 68, 88 (see The Pope)
Pizan, Christine, de, 139n
Plutarch's Lives, 23
Pompilia (character), 2, 3, 8, 9, 13,

14, 15, 16, 17, 18, 19, 20, 23, 42-62, 68-87, 88-98, 101-21, 125-34; despair, 79-80, 96, 127; divorce, 84-86, 133; forgiveness, 86-87; Incarnation, parallel with, 106-108; God's image, as, 133-34; intuition, 82-84, 112; Marriage, Christ's idea of, 131-32, as prostitution, 46-49, as rape, 50-62, ideal of, 113-16; priesthood, appreciation of, 72-74, 77-79, 80-85, 103-104, 108, 114-15, 117-18; radical innocence, 68, 118; womanhood, as celebration of, 133-34
Pope, The (character), 9, 18, 21, 56, 61-62, 65, 67, 72, 73, 87- 98, 107-108, 118-121, 126, 131, 134; Euripides, 94-98; Genesis, 91-92; love, definition of, 106-107; Caponsacchi, estimation of, 92-94; understanding of Caponsacchi's love, 118-19; Pompilia, estimation of, 88-92, 134
Pornography, 6, 7, 37, 42, 56, 67, 101, 105; Food metaphor, 49, 51-52, 58, 127; Horse metaphor, 43, 55, 127, 128; the man's woman, 57-60, 67, 73, 125, 129-31, 133-34
Pregnancy, 80-81, 84-85, 90, 107-108, 110-111
Prostitution, 24, 34, 48-49, 68, 90-91

Raphael, 57, 69, 75
Rape, 14-15, 42-62, 67, 84-85, 95, 126-29, 133; romanticization of, 58
Raptu Helenae, De, 141n
Raymond, William O., 138n

Rescue theme, 3, 8-9, 126
Ring metaphor, 20-22, 23-25
Romano (character), 54, 81, 84, 90
Rome, 13, 16, 19, 32, 34, 56, 57, 61, 65, 71, 72, 81, 84, 94, 101, 110, 121
Romulus, 34
Royal Academy, 6
Royal Casanatense Library, The, 138n

Salvation, 45, 68, 80-81, 116-17, 132
Sand, George, 3-6, 135n
Satan, 16, 41, 42, 46-47, 87, 91, 93, 97, 104, 141n
Scalette Convent, 13
Schlegal, 94
Schüssler-Fiorenza, Elizabeth, 132, 142n
Sexual cynicism, 13, 17, 22-25, 35-37, 49-62, 66-67, 68-69, 76-77, 87-88, 90-91, 93-94, 101-106, 112, 115, 125-34
Shakespeare, William, 24, 39, 115
Shaw, George Bernard, 24
Showalter, Elaine, 142n
Smalley, Donald, 137n
Society, 2, 3, 4, 9, 13-18, 29-62, 65-68, 73, 76-77, 79, 87-98, 101-106, 109, 114-16, 125-34
Solon, 34
Sordello, 7, 9
Sources (*see* Old Yellow Book), other, 23, 125, 138n

Sullivan, Mary Rose, 141n, 142n
Symonds, Arthur, 133, 143n

Tertium Quid (character), 17, 101
Tertullian, 41-42, 133, 140n
Thompson, Patricia, 135n
Titian, 58, 111, 140n
Triple Soul, 97-98, 107-108, 120-21
Truth, 17, 18, 20-25, 45, 48, 60, 68, 77-78, 83-84, 87, 91, 93, 97-98, 101, 104, 109, 111, 112, 113, 115, 116, 125, 132
Tuscany, 14, 31, 35, 57

Vasari, Giorgio, 24
Vellacott, Philip, 95, 141n
Venus, 67, 102, 140n
Virgil, 96
Virginity, 50, 114-15
Virilism, 53, 54, 129
Violante (character), 42

Wedgwood, Julia, 3, 22, 66, 129-30
Women, 3, 6-7, 8-9, 13, 15, 32-62, 66-67, 74-77, 88-98, 105, 108-109, 110-21, 125-34
Women's suffrage, 1
Woolf, Virginia, 139n

Yeats, William Butler, 15

Zeus, 96

A NOTE ABOUT
THE AUTHOR

Ann P. Brady is professor of English at Gustavus Adolphus College. In addition to numerous articles and book chapters, she is the author of *Lyricism in the Poetry of T. S. Eliot* (1979).